a Slice of Belgium

ERIC BOSCHMAN & NATHALIE DERNY
ADAPTED INTO ENGLISH BY ANTONY MASON

CW01573177

© belgiumtheplaceto.be TM - J Jeanmart

© belgiumtheplaceto.be TM – © Jon Martin

Contents

Chef Pascal De Valkeneer from Le Chalet de la Forêt
© belgiumtheplaceto.be - TM J. Brunton

© WBT - JP Remy

© belgiumtheplaceto.be TM - J Jeanmart

A Slice of Belgium:

a Slice of Heavenly Bread, a Slice of Life – two Slices of a Country…

This book is an invitation to adventure. An adventure in space – in Brussels, and in Wallonia, southern Belgium, almost Latin in its welcome and spirit of generosity. Also an adventure in time, looking back with fondness to the era of our grandmothers (and it will soon become apparent that the authors and most Belgians seem to share the same grandmother). For this book is essentially about a nostalgia for the flavours and smells, the sensations and feelings of childhood.

And that's fair enough, because it is, after all, grandmothers who are the guardians of the secrets, both small and large, of great culinary traditions – the roots of what is sometimes called, somewhat pompously, Gastronomy.

A Slice of Belgium is the English adaptation of the Belgian bestseller *Le Goût des Belges*, and if we have chosen to present to you just two of the three main regions that Belgium has to offer – Brussels and Wallonia (and what a tasty slice that is!) – it's not just because we have noticed how much the authors, and indeed the Belgians in general, refer to the distinctive food of these regions, but also because we truly believe that this celebration of their gastronomy is one of the most interesting and pleasurable ways to get to know them. They are, after all, two regions that are frequently misunderstood, if known at all, by the world at large.

Even Brussels, despite its international standing, needs such a spotlight, for too often it is dismissed as some kind of 'Eurocratic bunker', albeit that this image bears little resemblance to the reality of the city and the surrounding Brussels region, or its citizens.

As for Wallonia, it could not be more different from the rather unflattering stereotypes casually attributed to Belgium by those who don't know it. Flat, grey and boring, did I hear you say? Wallonia is anything but. And to convince you of that, we will provide you with brief introductions to its five provinces, describing what sets them apart, and where most visitors go and stay, to help you organise your next voyage of discovery and adventures in taste. Just a few hours from London or Calais, it's a place that will surprise you, refresh your spirits, and welcome you with open arms.

Françoise Scheepers, *Director of the Belgian Tourist Office Brussels & Wallonia for the UK & Ireland*

© belgiumtheplaceto.be TM - J Jeanmart

Food for thought:
is Wallonia a kind of cake?!

by
Eric Boschman

Gastronomy is never, ever a question of nationalism nor politics. It is, by definition, borderless, stateless, without frontiers. Just imagine that the moment you season a piece of meat you are stepping outside local boundaries, because here in Wallonia, for example, you are not going to find many exotic pepper plants growing on the rolling hills of Quenast or Petit-Rechain. And I have not even begun to ask where the salt comes from...

However, if Brussels is already an internationally renowned place for her gourmet qualities, I feel the urge to tell you more about the other part of Belgium, Wallonia, less known outside of the country borders and neighbouring regions…

How to evoke the flavours of Wallonia?
To begin with, let us start talking about its accents, its dialects. There are as many accents as regions in Wallonia, as many flavours as accents. People that come here for the first time have the impression that the locals here have roots which grow in their throat, just behind their taste buds. And it is the flavours and tastes from their various regions that little by little, form their words for them when they speak. Few people know, but, like many ethnic groups, the Walloons have a unique way of saying certain letters in their French-speaking alphabet: the inhabitants of Liège breathe out the H, the 'caroloregiens,' as the people of Charleroi are known, pronounce the A in a different manner, while the 'borain tamboureur' accent of people living around Mons tends to roll its R's. So the Walloon language is different but equally is also the same. Why? Because here in our country, everything always happens around a table, a bar, a mug of beer, a pint, a drink, a cup of coffee or a 'vitoulet' veal meat ball.

Wallonia is a land of welcome, transit and meeting places, which throughout the ages has been crisscrossed by numerous invaders who have all left their mark. But to its great profit, the region has successfully transformed what could have been indelible scars into unique tastes and flavours. So in the same way that the Walloon language has been influenced by different migrant groups, so has the traditional gastronomy here. That said, when Wallonia first comes to mind, let us be honest, people do not immediately think about gourmet cuisine. The far more likely responses are the people's wonderful sense of conviviality, the love of partying, festivals, surrealism, beer, woods prowling with wild game. But not 'haute gastronomie'. That august term is reserved for the chefs of Catalonia or Denmark, the ancient traditions of Tuscan cooking, certain regions of France. And yet, for visitors that make the effort to discover the hidden corners of Wallonia, there is a local speciality waiting to be discovered at the end of every off-the-beaten track, a tempting aroma wafting out the window of a kitchen.

The cuisine here is surprisingly cosmopolitan because the region's traditions and flavours have roots that spread all over Europe, because Wallonia is above all eclectic, a committed European, almost always at the edge of a frontier, open towards the world and all neighbours. And this openness has produced a culture of hedonism that is a permanent fixture in people's genes, so much so that many would risk eternal damnation just for a good meal! Why? Because here in our country, everything happens around a table, a bar, a mug of beer, a pint, a drink, a cup of coffee or a 'boulet' meatball in a rabbit sauce .

Walloon gastronomy is built on a foundation of incredible richness, something utterly rare, authentic, and unique. This is because the 'saveurs,' the tastes and flavours of our cuisine, are both local and cosmopolitan, because Wallonia is at the crossroads of dozens of different influences and trends from across the whole of Europe.

Travelling around the region there are wonderful bars and restaurants in every small village or big city, places where you >>

eat simply and where the menu features essentially local specialities. This is what our French neighbours have christened the cuisine of the "terroir". But, here in Wallonia, there is no way that "terroir" refers just to the geographical location. For us, "terroir" is not limited to the climate, a specific place, the ground, or even what is beneath the ground. Here we understand the soil, but for us, "terroir" is above all a human concept.

Many chefs here are Belgians who have immigrated from overseas, and it is this capacity for integration that is one of the strengths of Wallonia. This is something that you witness every day at mealtime around the table in dishes that have a very Belgian interpretation of fusion cooking. So to start with, Italian cuisine in Wallonia has been subtly altered, little by little, to suit local tastes, while even North African recipes have been given a Walloon makeover. And added to this there are the influences of all the different nations that passed through here over the centuries, which have imperceptibly dripped into daily life. That is why it can be so difficult to explain, for example, to an inhabitant of Verviers that the origin of his rice tart recipe probably comes from Venetian cuisine, or to try and tell a chef from Chimay that his escaveche comes from Persia. You will probably find yourself in the midst of a furious uproar with everyone jabbing toothpicks, raising their fists, and accusing you of the heinous crime of daring to question the local origin of the dish. What is important in Wallonia is not where the original recipe comes from, but how the locals have adapted it and made it their very own. Why? Because here in our country, everything always happens around a table, a bar, a mug of beer, a pint, a drink, a cup of coffee or an "avisance" minced sausage in pastry.

Although Walloon gastronomy still has to achieve the ethereal heights of 'haute cuisine', there is a band of talented chefs who have started along that long, tortuous road, shining a beacon into the future for the next generation. Unfortunately, there just is not that essential intellectual component that is so necessary to achieve international recognition for what these brave chefs are doing. And there are even a host of interesting things to discover in what can only be called Walloon fast-food, such as the "mitraillette," an irresistible French-fries sandwich, that has become a veritable cultural symbol for teenagers. But best of all is the good old Sunday lunch, served in a typically unpretentious restaurant, where the menu features the latest in fashionable food, but without all the hoopla and publicity generated by anorexic press attachées dressed all in black, even if she isn't wearing Prada high heels. What these simple, homely restaurants have been practising for decades is the now hip term known as 'locavorism', or more commonly, carbon zero consumption. But for them it is nothing exceptional, it is just daily life. In the town square of Nivelles everyone eats chard flans "Al d'jote", while over in Saint-Hubert, the local speciality is charcuteries from the Ardennes. It is all so obvious. Why? Because here in our country, everything always happens around a table, a bar, a mug of beer, a pint, a drink, a cup of coffee or a "pipe gaumaise" dry sausage.

Once you get to know the flavours of Wallonia you will love them and never forget them, because you have discovered these unique tastes; they stay with you, impregnated on your taste buds. The person who has never sipped an Orval beer on a rainy day in autumn, sitting beside a warm fireplace, his elbow resting on a thick black wooden table, wearing a sopping sweater after a walk in the beating rain, does not really know what our region is all about. The person who has never devoured a "truite au bleu" poached trout, accompanied by a glass of dry white wine, maybe from the nearby vineyards of Belgian Luxembourg, on a spring day when an elusive sun hesitates to dart its rays for fear their tips will be frozen off, does not really know where our area is. The person who has never heard the rat-a-tat of a carnival drum echoing from wall to wall through the narrow streets of a small town on a freezing cold morning on Shrove Tuesday, before eating, shivering, a "pistolet à l'américain" beef tartare sandwich, does not really know what is a true carnival. Because here in our country, everything always happens around a table, a bar, a mug of beer, a pint, a drink, a cup of coffee or a Gille de Binche.

© belgiumtheplaceto.be TM - J Jeanmart

© belgiumtheplaceto.be TM - J Jeanmart

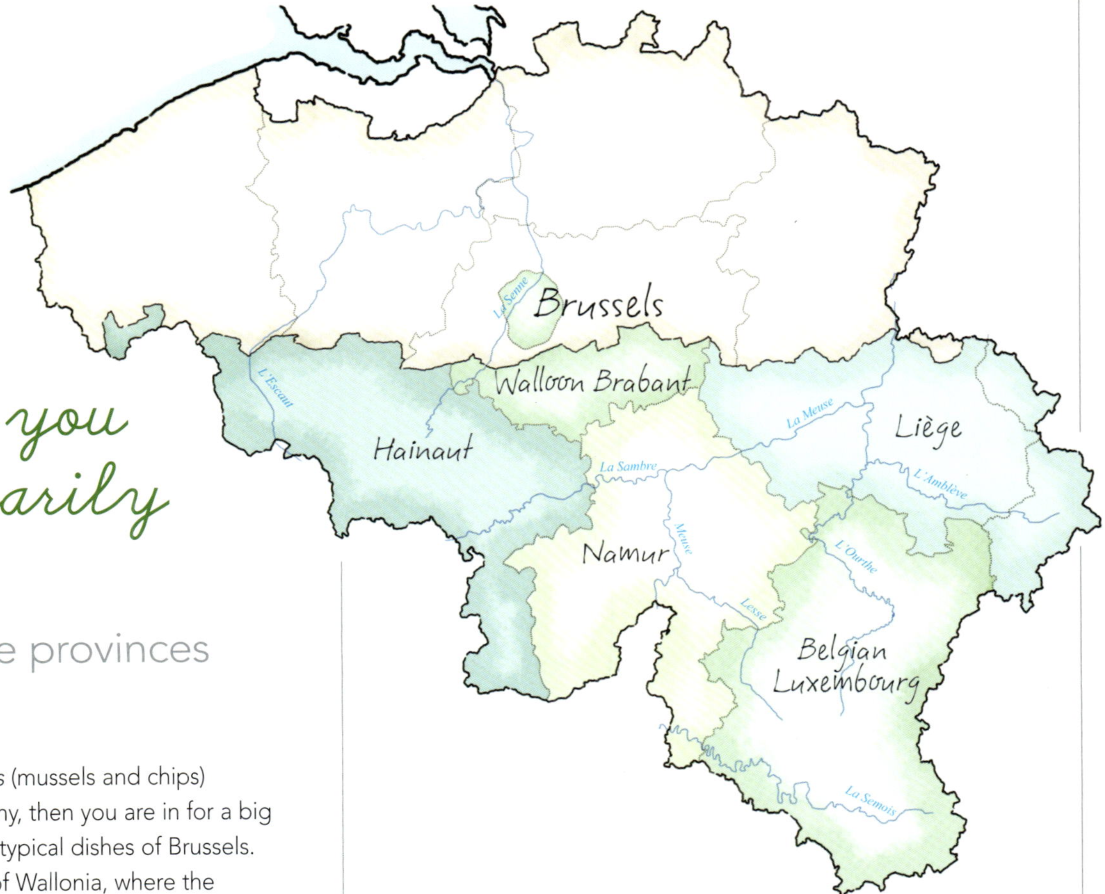

Belgium as you don't necessarily know it

Brussels and the five provinces of Wallonia

If ever you thought that *moules-frites* (mussels and chips) is the sum total of Belgian gastronomy, then you are in for a big surprise. That's just one of countless typical dishes of Brussels. And we haven't even begun to talk of Wallonia, where the gastronomy is as rich and varied as its astonishing landscape. And another big surprise: *moules-frites* isn't really Belgian at all – but you'll have to read on to find out why.

© belgiumtheplaceto.be TM - J Jeanmart

To guide you around the delights of this part of the country, we have subdivided the book into several parts, in two categories:

1. Geographically: Brussels, and the five provinces of Wallonia: Walloon Brabant, Hainaut, Namur, Liège, and Belgian Luxembourg.

2. Thematically, or by speciality: gourmet food, junk food (we are honest to a fault!), cheese, alcoholic drinks and non-alcoholic drinks, and so on.

The map will help you to visualize the gastronomic itineraries that you will be inspired to plan, as your mouth waters and your imagination takes fire.

So... bon voyage and bon appétit!

1. Specialities of Brussels

City, capital (five times over!)* and a region all of its own, Brussels is certainly three-dimensional!

More than 130 different nationalities can be found in Brussels.

Before Belgium existed as a nation, Brussels was the capital of the Duchy of Brabant, one of the most powerful in Western Europe.

Although, historically and politically, the Duchy of Brabant was quite separate from Dutch-speaking Flanders, the Bruxellois dialects (there are quite a few!) are a mix of Dutch and French. In the 18th century, however, the middle classes of Brussels opted to prioritize French: a practical decision perhaps, as French, the lingua franca of the day, was no doubt useful to facilitate international trade, but it also carried the promise of social elevation. Nowadays some 97% of Brussels citizens are French-speaking.

The Dukes of Brabant and the inhabitants of their capital had their job cut out to deal with a string of invaders over the course of their long, roller-coaster history: the Spanish, Austrians, French and Dutch have all occupied Brussels, and altered every aspect of it, down to the bottom of their kitchen pans.

This cross-fertilization was inevitable given Brussels's strategic position at the crossroads of all the major European cultures; its proximity to the sea port of Antwerp (a city also ruled by the Dukes of Brabant in medieval times), which provided a gateway to the world's sea routes; and its direct access to overland and river-based trade routes to the south – all of which were bound to produce a city with a hearty, hybrid approach to living, cooking and hospitality.

Brussels has taken full advantage of its access to the North Sea to embellish its culinary traditions with all kinds of seafood – of which mussels are just one. But it also has *cuisine de terroir*, cooking traditions shaped by the local landscape and its produce. This has a robust and earthy character, calling to mind the magnificent Brabançon draught horses which in the past brought the produce to the very heart of the city.

Today Brussels has a population of 1.5 million. Compared to Paris or London, that makes it relatively small, but make no mistake: it's got all the attributes of a major metropolis: cultural vitality, cosmopolitan attitudes, multilingual skills at every level. Notwithstanding, it has been able to preserve its human scale, a 'liveability' that has been lost in other capitals – a quality of life which arouses a touch of envy in the inhabitants of many other European capitals. The population density is one of the most telling indicators: Brussels has 7,000 people per sq km; Paris, 21,000.

After an absolutely must-see pilgrimage to the Grand' Place – the 'world's most beautiful theatre', as Jean Cocteau put it – you have to broaden your field of vision a bit to discover more of the charms of Brussels. Once you have been to the Sablon district, head on into the Upper Town and beyond: Avenue Louise, the Ixelles ponds, the area around Place du Châtelain, with its Art Nouveau and Art Deco flourishes. In the Lower Town, explore the Quartier Dansaert and the Place Sainte-Catherine, the former site of the fish market linked directly by canal to the North Sea.

*Capital of Belgium, Capital of the Brussels Region, Capital of the Flemish Community of Belgium (3% of the population of Brussels is Dutch-speaking, but the Brussels Region is bilingual, according to its constitution), Capital of the Wallonia–Brussels Federation (formerly the French Community of Belgium) and Capital of the European Union.

Each of the city's areas has its own distinct character:

- Cutting-edge designers: Quartier Dansaert
- International chic: Quartier Louise, Boulevard de Waterloo and Avenue de la Toison d'Or
- Bohemian-chic: Le Châtelain
- Bohemian-cool: Quartier St-Jacques (around the Rue du Marché au Charbon)
- African groove: Matongué
- Nostalgic 60s: St-Boniface
- Oriental vibe: Gare du Midi and Molenbeek

What follows are a few ideas to tingle your tastebuds, and get you looking beyond the usual menu card.

© belgiumtheplaceto.be TM - O Knight

Mussels – les moules

Mussels in Brussels? That's odd really, when you think about it. And we are not talking about our great Hollywood movie star Jean-Claude Van Damme here. The tradition of seafood generally is a bit odd, given that Brussels is about 100 km from the coast. But head to the Place Sainte-Catherine, still the focal point of our capital city's fish restaurants, and you begin to see why. This was once the head of the Willebroek Canal, completed in 1561, which led to the River Rupel and thence the River Scheldt, Antwerp and the North Sea, from which came a relentless supply of fresh seafood. Place Sainte-Catherine served as Brussels' fish market for a century until 1955.

But mussels – my goodness me, what a business, what a business! We have really made a meal of it! Mussels have become a question of national pride – nay glory! More than with the Red Devils (the national football team), more than with Eddy Merckx (the world's greatest ever cyclist, bar none), more than with Justine Henin (who brought unparalleled grace to the tennis court), we nail our colours to the mast with *moules*. Yet – here's the paradox – not one, not one single measly mussel, comes from Belgium! The mussels of which we are so inordinately proud – with their pearly, smooth and supple flesh – come for the most part from the province of Zeeland in the Netherlands.

For two simple reasons: the first is that mussels are produced there on an industrial scale, as a consequence of the second reason: the Dutch have, for a number of years now, pursued a wise and far-reaching policy of water-quality control in the Eastern Scheldt estuary. No waste water, no chemical runoffs from agricultural land. These strong-arm tactics have paid off, and as a result we eat tonnes and tonnes of their mussels. To add insult to injury, there is now a new vogue for *moules de bouchot* – from France. Smaller, meatier,

© belgiumtheplaceto.be TM - J Jeanmart

with a flesh that is more orange, and more expensive, they are produced in Normandy on vertical wooden stakes *(bouchots).*

Restaurants in Brussels serve *moules* by the bucket, in all kinds of guises, but essentially steamed in a shallow broth. Best to keep it simple, in my view: *moules marinière,* steamed with chopped celery, onion and parsley. Served with chips *(frites),* it goes without saying. And I won't brook any argument: mussels are eaten with the fingers. You may use a fork to extract the first, but thereafter you use the empty shell like a pair of pincers. You can also use a half shell like a spoon to drink the cooking liquid. Try softening the chips a little in the liquid too, to render them just that little bit more delicious. There are some who will also dip bread into the liquid, but, well, that's just perverse.

Le Stoemp – pronounced stoomp

You pronounce it 'stoomp'. *Stoemp, stoemp, stoemp!* It's the very sound of mashing potatoes. And that's just what a *stoemp* is, and in Belgium a stoemper is the instrument you use to do it – a potato masher. This is the kind of dish known as a *'plat consistant'* – solid, nourishing, comfort-food. In fact they may as well have invented that term for *stoemp*, so comfortably does it fit the label. It's classic popular cuisine, made with cheap, common ingredients, yet it has steadily grown in respect and status in recent years, part of a trend to revisit old traditions, so now *stoemp* often features on brasserie menus, even if it is not exactly the kind of dish you would imagine ordering outside the home.

The base is our old friend the potato. In Belgium the variety of choice is usually Bintje, the famed *frite* potato, but the vegetable that is mixed in with it will vary according the whim of whoever is cooking. Chopped carrots, cabbage and leeks are common companions, but usually only one of these: this is not a garden-produce mash-up. That said, sometimes chopped bacon bits are added to bring a bit of edge to the flavour. A good *stoemp* is a great accompaniment to *boulettes* (meatballs), sausages and *boudin noir* (soft black pudding, or blood sausage) – all washed down by a good Belgian beer.

© belgiumtheplaceto.be TM - J Jeanmart

Tomatoes stuffed with brown shrimps – Les Tomates-crevettes

If there is one dish that the Belgians might have every reason to detest, it's this: *les tomates crevettes,* too often made on the cheap with tasteless Dutch tomatoes, Dutch shrimps and industrial mayonnaise, with prewashed salad from France. Heavens above! this is virtually our national dish. Weird people the Belgians, sometimes, really. But the national origins of the ingredients are neither here nor there: to those who love this dish it's the quality of the ingredients that count. And their subtle and magical blend of flavours: the fruitiness of the tomatoes, the soft vinegariness of the mayonnaise, and the subtly peppery characteristics of the shrimps – which have to be the gorgeous North Sea *crevettes grises* (see page 78). Anything beyond that is hateful embellishment. Except chips *(frites),* of course. A *tomate crevettes* without chips feels like a beach holiday where something is missing, like a seawall without gulls, a week without sunshine, a kite that's broken free of its string. Unless, of course the *tomate crevettes* is part of your diet regime. But you would have to be ill for that.

© belgiumtheplaceto.be TM - J Jeanmart

Les Choesels – pronounced Shoesel

You might hear these called *choesels à la bruxelloise,* but that's a tautology: *choesels* can only be from Brussels. When Brussels was bustling in the early 1900s – when *'Bruxelles bruxellait',* as Jacques Brel put it, with women in their crinolines and men in top hats – this was *choesels'* hour of glory. And it was a glory that was pretty much confined to the capital, but what country doesn't like to hold its capital city at arm's length? In some *caberdouche* (crusty old tavern) of yesteryear, you may still find an ageing *ket* (fellow), with eyes as cloudy as his *lambic* beer, waxing lyrical about this dish in days gone by. There are precious few restaurants these days that still make *choesels* the traditional way – which possess the necessary skills to turn offal into a dish fit for a feast. But there was a time when every restaurant served *choesels* as now they serve sole. It was on every menu. It was an integral part of the food landscape of Belgium, or at least of the part occupied by the Brusseleirs. *Choesels* are not – as some ignorant folk suggest – bulls' testicles. That's just a popular rumour, designed to frighten children and lovelorn young women.

Rather, *choesels* are made of chopped calves' sweetbreads (pancreas), with a host of other bits of offal thrown in. Calves' sweetbreads are too precious to be used for the whole recipe, but with no sweetbreads, no *choesels*. So oxtail and liver, thymus gland sweetbreads, and the feet of a range of livestock also enter the equation. Preparation is laborious and has to be meticulous, or else the feast ends up as a *bazoef* – like an unappetising dish of leftovers. For the prize for the best accompaniment, try a side dish of fresh garden vegetables along with *lambic or gueuze* – the great Bruxellois beers – or a glass of Madeira, and let them fight it out.

© Lionel Louckx - Viva Mboma

Le Bloedpens – pronounced blued-pens

Bloedpens – or bloempanch in good *Brusseleir* (a.k.a. Bruxellois) – is a kind of black pudding, or *boudin noir* as we say in French, but it is not like any other. You only have to look at it to see this. First off, there is its size – a lot bigger than a *boudin noir,* even the ones made for Christmas. Then there are the lumps of whitish stuff which stud the slices. All of which requires a bit of explanation. As I intimated above, *bloedpens* is a Brussels speciality, the origin of which goes way back in time. It has been given a string of colourful nicknames, such as *'bifteck à carreaux'* or *'bufsteik mè roeite'* (chequered or tiled steak). Essentially, like all black puddings, you need pork blood, and intestines for the shape. With *bloedpens,* however, these are not pork intestines but beef, which give the thing its impressive girth, and the look of a steak when sliced. The white lumps are chunks of pigs' head: cartilage and bits of the ears and snout. Bacon pieces and bacon rind also get a look in. Nothing for weightwatchers and dieters here!

It needs something to bind it all together. For classic *bloedpens,* that's buckwheat flour, and nothing else will do. Spices, such as cinnamon and nutmeg, and various herbs give extra lift to the flavour.

Bloedpens is eaten cold, in slices, or warm and loosely mashed with a fork. In an *estaminet* (traditional tavern), a good beer is the essential companion, of course.

© belgiumtheplaceto.be TM - J Jeanmart

Les Caricoles or Whelks

Whelks are a Brussels speciality, even though the sea now longer laps around the Grand Place, having left the neighbourhood several tens of thousands of years ago. Known as *caricoles* locally, they have a firm place in the hearts of *kets* (guys) of Brussels' traditionally working-class *ville* basse (the lower town), the historic centre. In the *ville haute* (the upper town), around the Royal Palace, they walk around with their noses in the air and wouldn't know how to eat a *caricole*.

The habit of eating whelks really stamped its mark on Brussels gastronomy in the 16th century, when the Willebroek canal linked the city to the North Sea. Still today, in certain fixed locations, you can find stalls containing a huge enamel cauldron, with a stick of celery emerging from its steaming, aromatic broth. This is where the whelks are cooked.

Contrary to a rather idiotic rumour, *caricoles* have nothing to do with winkles (*bigorneaux* in French). *Caricoles* are whelks, basically sea snails (*bulots* is the usual French term); winkles are winkles. One is big, the other small; one comes in a crusty fawn shell, the other in a little black shell. The only thing they have in common is they are both delicious, if well prepared.

The word *caricole* is apparently closely related to the Belgian-French and Bruxellois word *crolle*, meaning a curl. It seems that whelks were called *caricoles* after the elaborate coiffures of Spanish ladies, during the days when Belgium was part of the Spanish Netherlands (until 1714). Yes, indeed, we were Spanish once.

You eat *caricoles* standing up, around the stalls. First remove the *opercule* (operculum, the hard little lid that covers the flesh) – if not, ycch! Then you go with your little fork to hoick the beast out of its

shell. Gently does it, to extract it all in one. You can drink the soup, but these days it is often highly spiced with chilli. During the famous Foire du Midi – which takes place every year, mid-July to mid-August, around the Midi station – on one side you have the fairground rides, and the other the *auvents* (stalls with awnings) selling mussels and all kinds of very local specialties, such as *boestrink aux caricoles* (smoked herring with whelks). It's an excellent place to witness another side of the city, far from the sanitised, wealthy, residential areas and the transitory European functionaries. Here it teems with people from all over the world discovering how the Bruxellois – to adapt Jacques Brel – can smell their beer to the heart of their *frites*.

Brussels Waffles –
Les gaufres de Bruxelles

Billions of bilious blue blistering barnacles! Anacoluthons! Nyctalops! Waffle irons!

It's no wonder that Captain Haddock regularly punctuates his conversation with a reference to waffles – at least in the Belgian editions. Either you're Belgian or you're not. Hergé, Tintin's creator, most certainly was, and if I'm not mistaken the great sea captain became so by default through his empathy with the hero.

And probably also for his love of *gaufres* (waffles). For while waffles are not exclusively Belgian, in Belgium, be they *gaufres de Bruxelles* or *gaufres de Liège* (see page 56), they are indisputably the most delicious in the world. And that's not to forget the hosts of other waffles that roam our lands: *gaufres de Verviers, de Namur, du Perron* (another type from Liège), *gaufres fines de Herve*. And that's not the half of it.

Brussels waffles – *gaufres de Bruxelles* – are light, frothy and crisp, and larger than their denser counterparts from Liège. They are eaten hot, sprinkled with icing sugar and covered – according to taste – with Chantilly cream, fresh fruit or chocolate. After an exhausting family day out shopping they bring joy to children and adults alike, especially, but not only, in winter.

In the past, it was these *gaufres de Bruxelles* that could be found on the corner of every street. We ate them wandering along the pavements, a ray of sunshine sparkling in ours eyes, a smile upon our lips. The shower of white that adorned one's lapels and the tips of one's fingers was all part of the charm.

La Roue d'Or in Brussels
© belgiumtheplaceto.be TM - Jeanmart

Comic Strip Wall Brussels
© belgiumtheplaceto.be TM - J P Remy

2. Specialities of the Province of Walloon Brabant

There was a time when there was just one Province of Brabant, but the constant and complex evolution of Belgium's governmental structure led, at the end of the 1980s, to its division into two, one called Flemish Brabant and the other – the subject of our interest for this book – Walloon Brabant (Brabant Wallon in French).

Walloon Brabant has been nicknamed the 'Garden of Brussels'. Certainly the green landscape that greets anyone leaving Brussels is remarkable for its beauty and intensity. One of the first châteaux of several you might pass is the Château de la Hulpe and its magnificent park, a favourite place for an outing for the Bruxellois. These days it's administered by the Solvay Foundation. The chemist, industrialist and philanthropist Ernest Solvay was one of the most remarkable of all Walloons: his invention of an industrial process to make sodium carbonate (used to make glass, film, detergent, dyes) has had a huge impact on the way we live. The Folon Foundation – set up to perpetuate the work of the internationally celebrated Walloon illustrator and sculptor, Jean-Michel Folon – has created its headquarters and museum close to the château. Film-lovers will remember having seen the château and its park in the superb film by the Bruxellois Gérard Corbiau called *Le Maître de Musique (The Music Teacher)* starring the great baritone – another Bruxellois with a world reputation – José Van Dam (not to be confused with the filmstar "Muscles from Brussels" Jean-Claude Van Damme!).

While we are on the subject of big names in Brabant, the most famous of all in the Province is without question Waterloo. No, it's not a village in France, nor a bridge or a railway station in London. It's a Belgian town a few miles south of Brussels. Waterloo owes its celebrity not to Napoleon but to the Duke of Wellington, for it was he who conscientiously and scientifically selected this undulating terrain to fight the final battle against the French Emperor. It's a place of myth and legend, where an unmissable series of events will take place in 2015, on the occasion of the battle's 200th anniversary.

Go there in the early hours of the morning, in summer, just as the sun starts to edge above the fringe of trees, while the morning mists have still not dispersed. And there you will see and understand the reasons for Wellington's strategic choice: the battle landscape of Waterloo, just like all of Walloon Brabant, gives a misleading impression of being flat, but in fact is full of subtle contours – just enough to get the edge on the enemy.

Brabançon farms, with their massive entrance arches and spacious working courtyards, are solid and endearing, like the draught horses that did their heavy work in the past. Several of those that witnessed the events at the Battle of Waterloo are still standing.

Nivelles lies a little further to the south. Its history dates back to Paleolithic times, but it really began to flourish under the Merovingians in the 7th century. The 11th-century collegiate church and cloisters of Saint Gertrude are masterpieces of medieval religious architecture.

© belgiumtheplaceto.be TM - J Jeanmart

The capital of the Province of Walloon Brabant is Wavre. A charming town of modest size, it has nonetheless been an important centre since the Middle Ages. Like Brussels, Wavre was a crossroads at the heart of the European trade network before the days of railways and motorways. This status also, alas, made it the theatre of bitter struggles and revolts against the successive occupations of Brabant by foreign powers.

The inhabitants of Wavre are nicknamed Maca, in reference to the bronze statue depicting a bare-bottomed little rascal trying to climb the low wall of the Hôtel de Ville (City Hall). Local tradition says that stroking his buttocks will bring good fortune for a year, but we leave that to you to verify.

Here are some Brabant specialities which all Belgians enjoy.

© OPT - JP Remy

Tarte al Djote –
pronounced tart al jott

If you don't want to look like the spy who came in from the cold whenever you're in the town of Nivelles, call it simply *une djote*. There are two varieties of *djote: 'verte'* (green) and *'mitoyenne'* which is half green and half white (the word means something like 'shared responsibility', which has some bearing, given that *Tarte al Djote* is not everyone's cup of tea).

The *verte* version is a mix of Swiss chard and *bètchéye* – little round lumps of cheese from Nivelles, otherwise known as *Boulette de Nivelles*. The white part does not absorb the Swiss chard, so the result is speckled. *Boulettes de Nivelles*, or the similar *Boulettes de Florenne*, or *de Romedenne* (all of which may be used to make *djote* in Nivelles), are cows' milk cheeses made with whole milk, and a traditional speciality of our region; elsewhere in Wallonia it is also known as *cassette*. The origin of the word *djote* may perhaps come from *jote*, the old word for Swiss chard (*bette* in French).

But whatever the origins of this typically Nivellois speciality, one ingredient that is essential is good butter, which is melted across the surface of the tart – because a *djote* has to be served *bin tchaude, bin blète è qu'èl bûre dèsglète* (hot, ripe and dripping with butter). You have to remember that in Nivelles on *n'a jamé stroné avè du bûre* (noone has ever been strangled by butter).

Djote has its fanatical supporters: more or less the entire population of Nivelles for a start. Others may be less convinced, at least to begin with. One thing is certain: if you are not native to that town, the first time you eat it, you don't forget it. Later, after your 250th *djote*, habit breeds affection. Needless to say, in Nivelles, and only there in the world, rather than ordering a home-delivery pizza, you can get a van to bring *djote* to your door. With a side-order of extra butter, please!

© belgiumtheplacetobe TM - J Jeanmart

Sweet memories of Napoleon

The Battle of Waterloo took place in 1815 on rolling farmland just to the south of the town of Waterloo. It was a great victory for Wellington and his Allies, but you can forget him. Napoleon, with his swagger and interesting love-life, stole the show and, despite his defeat, has become the brand-darling ever since. Buy the ashtrays, and the egg-cups, buy the sweets and the drink!

Yes, for all the fifes and drums, the uniforms, the hired soldiers and conscripts, the women of the baggage train, the sacrifices, we end up with Mandarine Napoléon. It's bizarre. This sweet liqueur seems to have nothing to do with all that marching about, except perhaps, when it came down to it, everyone ended up drunk. Somehow, anyhow, Mandarine has become a national speciality based on… mandarin orange peel, of all things.

How? Well the drink was created for Napoleon by the chemist and distiller Antoine-François de Fourcroy in about 1806, but it was only produced on a commercial scale after 1892, and later taken over by Fourcroy's descendants. It is now owned by the Dutch distillers De Kuyper.

And then there are *les bonbons Napoléon*. There are probably different colours now, I don't know – but for me they have to be yellow. Lemon yellow and with a real taste of lemon. The very definition of tangy. Round, so they hurt the roof of your mouth, and that's kind of annoying. Just how long do you resist before biting into them? I have never sucked a *bonbon Napoléon* to its core. But I have promised to put this to the test when Belgium celebrates its 200th birthday in 2030. To judge by the way things are going, by that time my teeth will be all implants and bridges, so I'll have to be content to suck anyhow. Meanwhile, if anyone discovers the time this sweet takes to melt completely, please let me know!

© belgiumtheplaceto.be TM - J Jeanmart

Cheese pie – la tarte au fromage

There is always a bit of *tarte au fromage* lingering somewhere in the memory of any Belgian's tastebuds. Some, like the *Tarte au fromage Namuroise* (from Namur), are fine creations of *fromage blanc* (a kind of cream cheese), beaten egg, caster sugar or brown sugar *(cassonade)* and a pinch of cinnamon. But the celebrated *Tarte au stofé de Wavre*, proud product of the town of Wavre, includes a layer of apple compote. The sweetness of sugared *fromage blanc* set against the acidity of *pommes reinettes* (pippin apples) are a part of our national and genetic heritage in taste – as Belgian as a cornet of hot *frites*.

The *stofé* itself is a mixture of low-fat *fromage blanc* and eggs, caster sugar or *cassonade*, and ground almonds. Purists may add ground almond macaroon biscuits soaked in rum overnight. The ultimate magic comes from the incorporation of fluffy, beaten egg-whites right at the end of the preparation of the cheese mix.

The pastry is first of all covered with a thin layer of apple compote, followed by the foamy cloud of beaten cheese. If here and there little pockets of pure *fromage blanc* persist, that's all to the good, as this adds character to the whole creation.

A *Tarte au stofé de Wavre* is never prepared singly: there they always make them in batches of three to five at a time: that's just how it's done. There's no doubt that making a good *tarte au fromage* calls for a certain skill. Eating one, however, presents absolutely no difficultly at all, beyond knowing when to stop.

© belgiumtheplaceto.be TM - J Jeanmart

Pork Chops, sauce Blackwell –

La côte de porc Blackwell

Shocked? Surprised? Perhaps you should be – but things may not be quite as bad as they appear. *Côte de porc Blackwell* is actually a brasserie dish *par excellence*.

It should really be *La Côte de Porc Cross et Blackwell*, as it takes its name from the pickles produced by the (originally) English company Cross & Blackwell, which was the foundation stone of a Belgian piccalilli tradition. 'The Original Piccalilli l'Étoile', made by l'Étoile sauce company of Wavre, is based on an original English recipe.

Correctly prepared, with the sauce delicately finished with cream after the pan has been deglazed with white wine, *Côte de porc Blackwell* is delicious. Especially with rissolé potatoes or chips: you can soften their crispy crusts and impregnate them to saturation point with the delicious yellow sauce. And of course, it's even better if accompanied by a blonde, for the conversation. (We're talking beer, here, of course.)

Overcooked and dried out, drowned in a sauce that has been overegged with mustard, that was my nightmare every Wednesday when I was studying. Happily, there were always the chips and the little pot of mayonnaise to take the edge off my hunger and my desires.

But this isn't the place for self-psychoanalysis, so I think I'll leave it there.

© belgiumtheplaceto.be TM - J Jeanmart

Mons © belgiumtheplaceto.be TM - J Jeanmart

P&V

3. Specialities of the Province of Hainaut

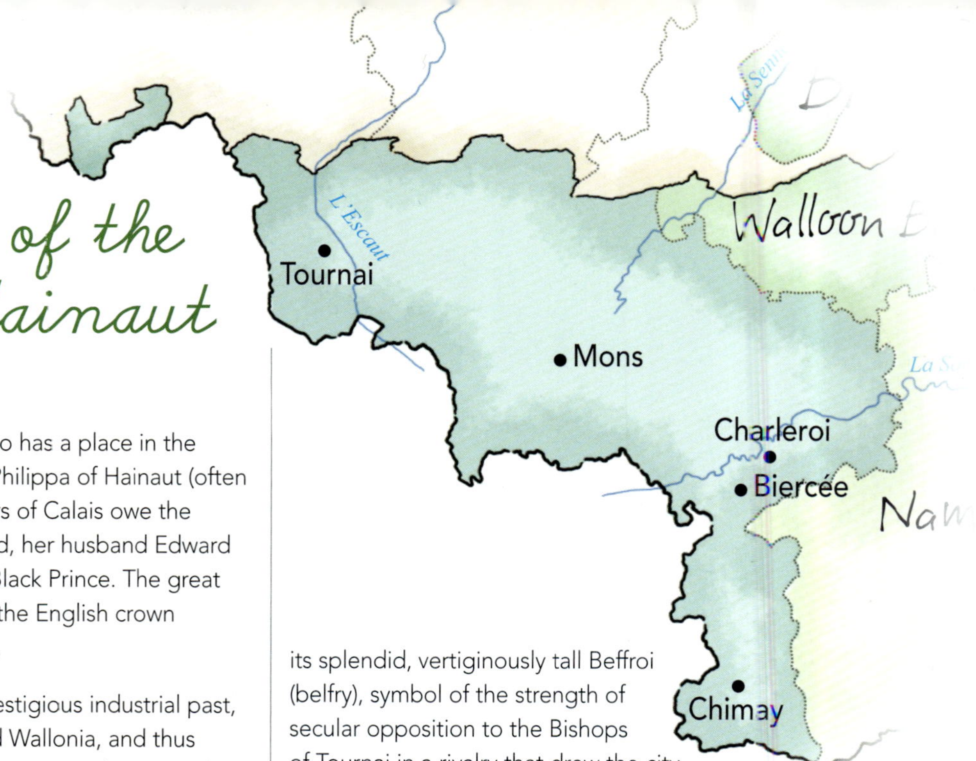

The rich history of the County of Hainaut also has a place in the chronicles of England. It is to kind-hearted Philippa of Hainaut (often spelled Hainault in English) that the Burghers of Calais owe the mercy shown to them by the king of England, her husband Edward III. She was the mother, too, of the famous Black Prince. The great medieval city of Tournai briefly came under the English crown (1513–18) after it was captured by Henry VIII.

In Belgium, Hainaut is also famous for its prestigious industrial past, which – along with the Liège Basin – hoisted Wallonia, and thus Belgium, into the top three industrial nations prior to the Second Wold War, alongside Britain and the USA. Today, the scars of this past have begun to recede and give way to nature. The landscape has rediscovered the green shades of its older self, and now it is becoming ever easier to imagine how this beautiful County once looked, with its fine historic towns and magnificent châteaux, such as Beloeil, Seneffe and Chimay.

Tournai and Mons – close the French border and just 1½ hours from Calais – are the most important medieval cities of the province. Tournai was the fount of what many people call 'Flemish Art', but which should really be known as 'Scaldian Art', after the River Escaut (or Scheldt) that passes through it on its way to Ghent and Antwerp – an art tradition that spread well beyond the boundaries of the old County of Flanders.

On a sunny summer's day, Tournai and its Grand'Place could be the Siena of the North. It has been doubly honoured by UNESCO as a World Heritage Site, once for its cathedral with its unique five bell towers, which alone illustrates the power of this first capital of the Kingdom of the Franks, where Childeric I founded his Merovingian Dynasty in the late 5th century AD; and again for its splendid, vertiginously tall Beffroi (belfry), symbol of the strength of secular opposition to the Bishops of Tournai in a rivalry that drew the city into the wars of religion in the 16th century. One of its evacuated Protestant offspring, Pierre (or Peter) Minuit, was responsible for the purchase of Manhattan in 1624 for the Dutch colony of New Amsterdam (later New York).

Mons, the capital of the Province of Hainaut, is situated just half an hour from Charleroi and its international airport, so very easy to get to. Mons owes its origins and name to the 'mount' on which the Romans founded a military base. It has maintained this theme into the modern world as the site of the NATO's Supreme Headquarters Allied Powers in Europe – SHAPE for short. Mons has also always been on the front line of technology. The model society imagined by the enlightened owner of the industrial colliery complex at Grand-Hornu, in the 18th century, and the hi-tech enterprises found in Mons today both bear witness to this. Added to this, Mons has now also put itself on the cultural front line, with the creation of a whole series of new art and

© belgiumtheplaceto.be TM - J Jeanmart

music venues which will be inaugurated in 2015, when the city will be celebrating its year-long role as a Cultural Capital of Europe. That will also be an opportunity to draw attention once more to its UNESCO-validated heritage: its historic Beffroi (belfry) and its remarkable industrial-era boat lifts; the Ascenseurs de Strépy, on the Canal du Centre; and the extraordinary festival, dating from 1380, held on Trinity Sunday (May/June), called the Ducasse de Mons (or Doudou), which culminates in the Battle of Lumeçon between St George and the Dragon.

To the British, Mons is also known as the place where the first military encounters took place in August 1914, and the legend of the Angels of Mons – ghosts of the archers of Agincourt led by St George (patron saint both of England and Mons), who miraculously came to the rescue of the beleaguered British forces in a night-time retreat. Mons marked the start and finish of Britain's war, for it was here that the first and last soldiers fell.

One last word about the Hennuyers (the people of Hainaut): jovial and kind (viz. the kind-hearted Philippa), they will welcome you openly and without undue fuss, a bit as if you were visiting your distant cousins. And always with some delicious local speciality to hand.

Tournai © belgiumtheplaceto.be TM - J Jeanmart

Toast à la Boulette

Do you know what a salamander is – or *salamandre* in French?

There are number of possible responses to this simple question. The first, and the most obvious, is that a salamander is a viviparous urodele amphibian which gets about by walking, not leaping like many of its other amphibian friends. That's the least helpful response with respect to Belgian food. Which is a pity for the poor old salamander, but you've got to draw the line somewhere, and sometimes you just have to lump it. The Salamandre is also a tower well known to the inhabitants of Beaumont, a charming little place in the south of Hainaut, a former garrison town which owes its name to its 'Bellus Mons' (Beautiful Hill in Latin), and which witnessed, a few centuries back, the painful tale of Les Trois Auvergnats: three thieves from the Auvergne in France who – as the legend recalls – mistakenly attacked Emperor Charles V, and were promptly hanged. Now, on the question of food, Beaumont might also appear as useless as the aforementioned salamander. But that would be a mistake, because Beaumont is also home of the Belgian macaroon. But that's another matter.

Back to the salamander. In the kitchen, in English and in French, it's a mini overhead grill designed specifically to brown and gild the tops of dishes – *gratins, crème brulée* and the like. It takes its name from a mythical animal used in heraldry, which has the capacity to resist fire. And here is why I raise the subject. My parents, a good thirty years ago now, opened a restaurant in the middle of nowhere. IN THE COUNTRY. Capital letters, big time. Nature, birds, rustic folk chewing on straws, the smell of cow dung. Since the country was the main selling point, the emphasis was on local produce. Having been to some degree an objective witness of the evolution of gastronomy through the decades, I can attest that today, with the development of modern agriculture, this is now virtually impossible. But let's go back to my parents. They insisted on farm-produced butter, farm-produced fresh cream (you should have seen the perplexed faces of customers when it separated in their coffee!), duck/goose/hen eggs from the village, and so on.

And *la boulette* – that famous cows' milk cheese made across a large portion of Wallonia. Sorry, 'was made' I should say, for reasons given above. Sold in the form of half a ball, this cheese is lumpy, has a smell that verges on the brutal, virile you might say. To make a virtue of this, my father had the bright idea to add a bit of fresh cream to the cheese, plus eggs, a little paprika and pepper, before slapping it like magma onto slices of bread. The combination was then subjected to the gleaming metal salamander, on the sides of which I could admire my adolescent acne while basking in the gentle heat that it radiated. The salamander that is, not my face. The toasted results were offered to customers before they embarked on sampling the local goat cheeses. Therein lies another story. Given the number of years that this ritual lasted, and the number of customers who ordered this week after week, I hope I might be forgiven for thinking that *le toast à la boulette* was an essential part of the gastronomic taste of a great number of Belgians.

Chimay –
Beer and cheese

As mentioned under Orval (see page 70), Chimay is one of the six great Trappist breweries of Belgium, producing divine beer under its different coloured labels, each with its own properties and strengths. I won't dwell on that here. Just try them and see if you, like me, are lost for words. I have an additional excuse too: being short of space, I'm going to concentrate on another aspect of Chimay: it's wonderful cheeses.

Whoever speaks of wine speaks of vines; whoever speaks of beer speaks of barley and hops; whoever speaks of cheese, speaks of cows. Nanny goats, ewes, mares, female yaks and rhinoceroses also give milk, but in Wallonia we are generally happy enough with cows. It's a just a matter of ease. To make milk you need cows, and to raise cows you need pasture. Ha! There's certainly enough of that around here!

The Trappist monks at the Abbey of Notre-Dame de Scourmont near Chimay have been making the stuff since 1876. Le Vieux Chimay apart, this is a semi-soft, uncooked cheese. There are four main types, each with its own characteristics. The *Grand Classique* is, to state the obvious, their great classic. It's made in wheels of 2.2 kg. With a rich and creamy texture, it has a flavour that evokes crusty bread, and milk fresh from the farm. *Chimay à la Bière* is, as the name suggests, finished with Chimay beer. While it ripens in the cellar, it is washed regularly and with Trappist love, which confers upon it an unmistakeable aroma of hops and fruit. The Grand Cru undergoes a longer period of ripening than the others. As for Vieux Chimay, this is a hard and dense, pressed cheese, matured for eight months, during which it acquires a delicious flavour of hazelnuts laced with a touch of bitterness. The monks devote a considerable amount of time to prayer, to reading (I am secretly hoping that this

© OPT/WBT

© belgiumtheplaceto.be TM - J Jeanmart

book is available in the abbey's library), to making their beer and cheese. The taste of the latter has changed a little over time to adapt to our Darwinian tastebuds, but it remains a traditional cheese, matured by hand by the monks in the vaulted cellars of the abbey. Which means it has unquestionably preserved its integrity and authenticity – and the kind of flavour that makes you sit up and listen.

Cramique – pronounced Craargh-mick

Cramique comes originally from the west of Belgium, from the area around Tournai known as the Tournaisis, but it's one of those foods that crosses borders, and gender. It's a masculine word in Belgium, but *la cramique* in France, or *outre-Quiévrain* as we say – to use a quaint old expression, Quiévrain being the crossing point on the old Brussels–Paris railway line. It seems that originally cramique was a cake-like bread that was made specially for local fairs and festivities. The raisins and the lighter dough are more recent arrivals.

In fact, the French and Belgian versions have evolved along separate paths, like dissimilar twins. In France, *la cramique* is a brioche-style pâtisserie, with some chocolate bits and raisins thrown in. Our *cramique,* by contrast, is a brioche-style bread with raisins. But forget the niceties: all that really matters is that our *cramique* is toasted, coated with salted butter and then dunked into a cup of hot chocolate when it's raining horizontally outside. Does life ever get any better than that? *Cramique* can also be eaten untoasted, but always with salted butter, to highlight the contrast. A fine slice of *cramique,* dreamily soft, spread with butter thickly enough to fill the holes, where the crumbs stick a bit to your teeth, and where you feel the cold of the butter against your gums… Hmmm.

In some hospitals *cramique* is given to patients on Sundays, as a kind of treat, a little taste of happiness. Speaking of which, *cramique* with margarine or with unsalted spreadable butter is forbidden under article 107d of the Geneva Convention. It is a flagrant abuse of Human Rights and Children's Rights. Apparently some home-economists and dieticians don't agree, but they are fighting a losing battle: *cramique* with salted butter will soon triumph over such dark forces of denial.

© belgiumtheplaceto.be TM - J Jeanmart

I have heard too – but have no irrefutable proof – that some outlandish tribes eat *cramique* raw, straight out of the bag. It's possible I suppose, and I can understand the temptation, so I keep my anthropological antennae switched on wherever I roam, hoping to pick up evidence of this strange phenomenon.

Macaroni with sugar – Les macaronis au sucre

I'm going to be telling you about the sweets and candy that coloured my childhood – so it occurs to me to tell you also about macaroni with sugar.

Les macaronis au sucre, of course, play no part in *la haute gastronomie;* in fact they have no connection to gastronomy at all. Here we connect them to Hainaut in honour of the hundreds of thousands of Italians who came to work in the coal mines and steel industry, especially after the Second World War – but that tenuous link was made only to fire our imagination as kids, called in from the garden to eat, with our trousers holed at the knees, unbrushed hair and ruddy cheeks.

At home we never got macaroni and sugar unless we first had macaroni cheese – or, to be more precise, *gratin de macaronis jambon-fromage* (cheese and ham; see page 118). These two dishes were inseparable. As inseparable at the table as my brother's grimaces whenever he had to eat (if first he could be caught) and my untameable appetite (I have not changed). After the macaroni cheese came the rest of the macaroni. Kept warm in a strainer left in the big saucepan, they patiently awaited their turn, confident and sure of their effect.

I think I remember Mother – who had done a book-based course with the celebrated Belgian chef and writer Gaston Clément (1879–1973) – always telling us at about the penultimate forkful of the gratin that there was still a bit of pasta left over, and if anyone was still hungry, if we wished, she would make them into *macaronis au sucre*. I don't know if we had time to reply before the little dessert plates appeared. There was no time to waste, for macaroni and sugar is a dessert that trumps all desserts.

You won't find a recipe for *macaronis au sucre*. It belongs to that class of simple family dishes that you never find in a book – which is why we are making an exception in this masterwork. Basically, it's just cooked macaroni and the light, fine-grained brown sugar that the Belgians call *cassonade*. But to make good *macaronis au sucre,* you have to think about the macaroni. The bigger the calibre, the greater the pleasure (even if your other half tries to reassure you otherwise). Cook them *al dente* (just short of soft). Let them rest while the *gratin* is consumed. Melt an enormous knob of good-quality, salted butter in a saucepan, then nimbly toss in the little beasts. As soon as they are hot, turn off the engine and pour on the sugar. Let it melt for a few minutes before serving. Serve. Factor in a high quantity tolerance for the children, because the bigger the calibre of the macaroni, and the more butter you add, and the sweeter the sugar-content, the more you can expect general mayhem and an outrageous smacking of lips.

Well, if you're doing it, it's got to hit the mark, hasn't it?

L'Eau de Villée

The Villée is a little stream that flows through the village of Biercée – a place that's a mere stone's throw from the UNESCO-World-Heritage-Site Belfry of Thuin. Or cherry-stone's throw away perhaps one should say, as cherries are a famous product of Biercée. The history of l'Eau de la Villée began a long while ago when someone from Normandy (home of Calvados), on a trip to see family in the village, advised them not to waste the windfall apples that lay around the trees, but instead to put them to good use by making *eau de vie* (brandy) from them. In 1946 a pharmacist called Jules Cleempoel converted a German torpedo tube, salvaged from the recent war, into a still. Which goes to show that you can turn swords into ploughshares. Biercée's *distillerie artisanale* was thus born, and to begin with it was used to make *eau-de-vie* from the various fruits brought in by local producers. In 1981 the new managers, Georges and Jany Pire, launched l'Eau de Villée, an alcohol made with lemon and four other fruit brandies. To start with, it was more of a *succès d'estime,* appreciated by the cognoscenti, but known only in the Charleroi region. I remember that when I was a kid, l'Eau de Villée was served in restaurants over ice with a zest of lemon and a mint leaf – and to forget the mint was an invitation to violent abuse, crime even. Since then the drink has become a popular commercial success, and it is no longer served as it was in those pioneering days. In 2000, the Distillerie de Biercée moved a short distance from Biercée itself to the 16th-century Ferme de la Cour at Ragnies, now a fully-fledged tourist attraction, producing not just l'Eau de Villée, but also a host of other fruit-based *eaux-de-vie* and gins.

© belgiumtheplaceto.be TM - J Jeanmart

Côte de porc al berdouille

Here's a pretty name to whet your appetite: 'Pork chops in mud'. But don't panic: while the Walloon word *berdouille* does indeed mean mud, this dish does not taste especially strongly of what lies beneath a third-division football goalkeeper's boots on a winter's day – it simply has the colour of his shorts at the end of the match. *Côte de porc al berdouille* is a classic dish from Mons and it's certainly not something you are likely to stumble upon on your weekend break in the South of France. Nevertheless, you may well come across it beyond the Mons city limits, and – who knows – be tempted to make it at home, having heard its praises sung here.

The basic ingredients are: margarine, butter, flour, stock, mustard, white wine, vinegar (traditionally white, or spirit, vinegar), gherkins, shallots, and a friendly pig who will provide you with some fine pork chops. Brown the chops in a pan using the margarine (not butter: that's how it's done in Mons). Now make the mud. For four chops, prepare a roux using 50g of butter and 50g of flour. Add 500ml of warm stock and whip together until smooth, and heat this – stirring constantly – to make a thickish sauce; season with salt and pepper to taste. Chop four shallots and fry them gently in butter; add 100ml white wine and 1 tablespoon of vinegar, and then the roux sauce plus 4 tablespoons of mustard and 3 medium-sized gherkins, chopped into fine slices. Heat through, and adjust the seasoning. When the chops are cooked, lay them on the plate and cover them with the sauce, and sprinkle over some more sliced gherkins.

It's a hearty dish that can be served with *frites* and a salad, and a good beer is *de rigueur*, of course. Or you can serve it with potato mash, which some say – when mixed in with the lumpy sauce – is the real inspiration for this dish's name.

© belgiumtheplaceto.be TM - J Jeanmart

Dinant © belgiumtheplaceto.be TM - J Jeanmart

4. Specialities of the Province of Namur

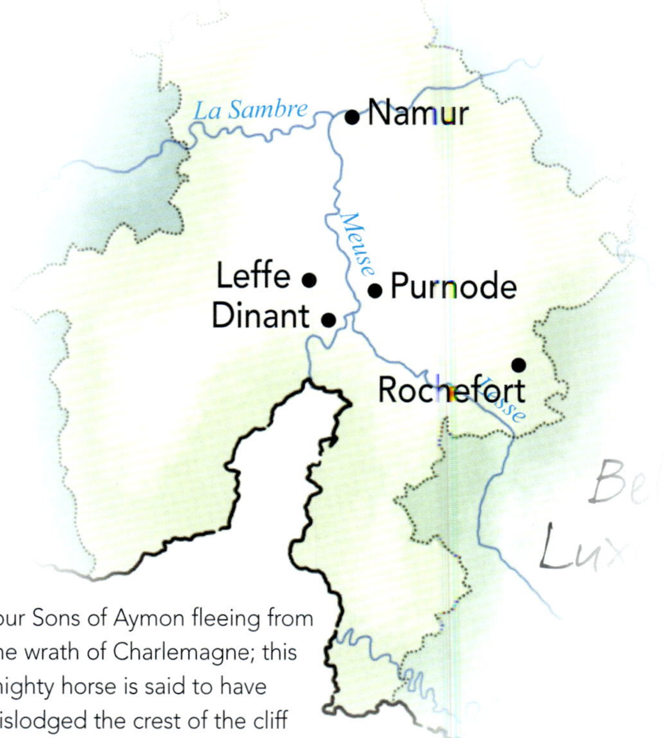

'O time, suspend your flight…' This line from the French poet Lamartine could find no better match than the Valley of the River Meuse, as it flows northwards from Dinant and swings east towards Andenne, passing Namur (capital of the region and the province) and Wépion (capital of Belgian strawberries) on the way. The beauty of the landscape and its light made this one of the favourite sketching locations of the painter J.M.W. Turner.

In the Province of Namur, everything seems softer, slower. It's a slowness which has made the snail the mascot of the city of Namur, and which is expressed even in the slight drawl in the Namurois accent (the actor Benoît Poelvoorde* is the exception that proves the rule).

The châteaux and their gardens (Freÿr, Annevoie), the castles (including the ruins of Poilvache and Logne, and the remarkable Corroy-le-Château), the citadels and fortresses (Dinant, Namur), the Belle Époque villas that adorn the banks of the River Meuse, the villages, among which are some of the prettiest in the whole country – all set against their backdrops of abundant greenery – make the Province of Namur one of the most attractive parts of Belgium. It makes a splendid gateway to the legendary hills of the Ardennes range, the Belgian part of which it shares with the Provinces of Liège and Belgian Luxembourg.

These architectural attractions run the course of the varied and fascinating history of this former County, as witnessed if you follow the River Meuse and the towns and villages along the 'Charlemagne Route'. A famous feature of Dinant – a very picturesque town tucked up against the chalk cliffs that flank the River Meuse – is a giant needle of rock called the Rocher Bayard, which, according to legend, was formed by the hoof of the Bayard Steed ridden by the four Sons of Aymon fleeing from the wrath of Charlemagne; this mighty horse is said to have dislodged the crest of the cliff while jumping across the river in a single giant leap. Later in time, Dinant became a possession of the Prince-Bishops of Liège, whose extensive territories straddled the midriff of modern Belgium. Later still, it produced one of its most famous sons, Adophe Sax, inventor (in the 1840s) of the saxophone, without which who knows what modern music would be.

Dinant too was one of the 'Martyr Cities' of the First World War, and a strategic pinch-point in the Second. It became the furthest point west reached by German forces in their desperate push to retake Brussels during the Ardennes Offensive in the winter of 1944/45, also known as the Battle of the Bulge.

Music lovers should note the annual music festival hosted by Namur in early July. The imposing Citadelle de Namur (a fortress designed by Louis XIV's ubiquitous military architect Vauban, as was Dinant's) is also often the setting for concerts and shows of high quality.

The centre of Namur, and its web of pedestrianized streets, is a dream for fashionistas, with a huge variety of high-quality shops selling clothes and, especially, shoes. This is no doubt due to a legacy of expertise left by its past as a city of tanners. The museum dedicated to the Namur's *enfant terrible*, the Symbolist illustrator and painter Félicien Rops, is worth looking out for, unless you are of prudish disposition: the steamy eroticism of some of his work edges close to hard porn, even bestiality. This aspect should not, however, be allowed to overshadow his real talent as a gifted and original draughtsman. The fact that the great French poet Charles Baudelaire entrusted Rops with the task of illustrating his masterwork *Les Fleurs du Mal* says it all.

Such ardour can easily be soothed when the magnificent Église Saint-Loup, a masterpiece of Baroque architecture, is open for a concert. Not to be missed, if the opportunity arises.

The vineyards of the Province of Namur were the first in Wallonia to be granted an Appellation d'origine controlée, in 2004, under the name Côtes de Sambre-et-Meuse, adding another jewel to the crown of a province already famed for its wide range of beers, including the 'abbey beers' of Leffe, Floreffe and Maredsous, and the sainted Trappist beer of Rochefort.

Footnote: *Namur-born Benoît Poelvoorde became internationally famous thanks to his first feature movie, the cult classic *C'est arrivé près de chez vous*, translated as *Man Bites Dog*, in which he starred, and which he co-wrote and co-produced. For a hilarious take on French vs Belgian stereotyping, see him in *Rien à Déclarer (Nothing to Declare)*, with Dany Boon.

© belgiumtheplaceto.be TM - J Jeanmart

Strawberries from Wépion – La fraise de Wépion

The town of Wépion is a tranquil suburb of Namur, where in season the banks of the River Meuse are beaded with strawberry growers' stalls. This may no longer be quite the sight that was captured in old prints, and nor indeed is the Meuse; the old stone houses have given way to more modern constructions, and Wépion has become a dormitory town for the big city rather than a picturesque Walloon village. But while the landscape of old has changed bit by bit, the agricultural tradition has remained. And here at Wépion it's all about strawberries. In schools the classrooms are painted red. In the shops the wrapping paper is decorated with strawberries. The letterhead of local municipal administration features a strawberry emblem, and the traffic lights have been shaped as giant fruits. No, I'm joking – but only so you might grasp the scale of this phenomenon.

Wépion strawberries are famed throughout Belgium. So what makes them so special? They are pert little creatures that live on the hillsides in the valley of the River Meuse, revelling in the light and a chalky soil that drains quickly. Like all the valley-dwellers here, they benefit from a daily dowsing of mist which – according to the growers – gives then their unique and lustrous characteristics. That's the *'terroir'* side of things; as for the human side, that comes in the form of polytunnels for the plants, planting and selection by hand, drip-feed irrigation, and the straw bedding that is laid down beneath the fruits. Given all this, life looks pretty good for a strawberry around these parts. Except for that wake-up call at 5 o'clock in the morning. To join its little sisters in the 500g punnets and be shepherded off to the points of sale or the auctions that take place every evening from mid-May to the end of July.

The only thing that one might regret in this tale is that the season does not last longer. That's how life goes: there are days with and days without, and usually more of the latter.

© belgiumtheplaceto.be TM - J Jeanmart

Snails – Les petits-gris

They are called *les petits gris* in French: 'the little grey ones': cherished edible snails. *Helix aspersa*. In Britain, that's the common garden snail. Yes, the very same thing… but, well, let's just say the British don't know what they are missing.

In Belgium there are several ways to get snails. The proactive method is to pull on your wellington boots, pick up a bucket and head off to the nearest railway embankment colonised by *petits gris*. The professional method is to breed them. You don't need a diploma or certificate, only a minimum of equipment and knowledge. I know a few people who raise snails in their garden; at most they have some lettuces, thyme and an apple tree. You need some kind of coop or cage where you can isolate and 'purge' the snails with a controlled diet for a week or so before eating them – but that's all you need. The lazy method is to buy them.

Generally frozen. It's child's play, but at least it's something, especially if Mum has presented you with a set of snail dishes, tongs and little forks along with a few bargain bottles of Gevrey-Chambertin and a pot of mustard in the wake of her recent trip to Burgundy. There is also, of course, a reliable gastronomic method: book a table at a good restaurant that knows what it is doing.

Snails are something of an institution in Namur. Well, the Namurois do have a reputation for being a bit slow… but, hey!, that's just a joke about they way they talk ('Naaaamur'). The snail tale dates back to the Middle Ages. Which reminds me: I must mention the famous snail races presented by street performers during the Fête de Wallonie, that takes place in Namur in September. It's worth going out of your way to see them.

Just as you should see the *petit gris* themselves, dripping with garlic butter and served in their shells, on in a potato salad. Accompanied by a dry white wine and a slice of good bread. For me, a couple of dozen is about right. Just to start with. Hmmm… What was I saying about the snail races?

© belgiumtheplaceto.be TM - J Jeanmart

Couques de Dinant

It goes without saying that if you go to Dinant, you've got to buy a *couque* – a hard kind of biscuit, moulded with all kinds of traditional shapes, pictures and designs, and in all sizes imaginable – some the size of a doormat. But to take one away, you need to respect several basic principles. First fundamental rule: don't think you are going to eat it. Equal first fundamental rule: don't be tempted to take a bite out of it, unless you fancy being called ' one-tooth' for as long takes to complete your orthodontic repairs.

The *couques* of Dinant can be eaten, but with caution. By the same token, herein lies the second rule: don't drop one on your foot unless you are wearing safety shoes. These beasts are hard, really hard. But smirk as much as you like: Dinant has the last laugh: these biscuits are sold in vast quantities and exported far and wide, even as far as Japan.

Couques de Dinant date from the 18th century, and the finer details of their production are a secret jealously guarded by a few companies in the town. While the recipe itself may not be complicated – they are essentially made of wheat flour (in the past from spelt wheat flour) and honey – the mystery lies primarily in the method of baking, passed down from one generation of *couquiers* to the next. In a similar way to *spéculoos* (see page 90), the *couques* are shaped in hand-carved wooden moulds. These moulds give the *couques* their extraordinary range of shapes and images, from a bunch of grapes to a classic panoramic view over Dinant from its historic Citadelle.

© couques collard

Crottes de Recogne

Ah, French culinary language, at once so refined and so crude. *Les crottes:* the word means droppings, as of rabbit or sheep. In other words, poo. You can find stinky cheeses called *Crotte du Diable* (Devil's poo), and similarly *crottins* of goat cheese. So what are *Crottes de Recogne?* Well, there are those days when everyone needs to show a bit of humility – even me. In order to give a full answer I reach for the encyclopedia. *Crottes… Crottes du Diable:* Nodules of calcium phosphate found in the Ardennes. Hmmm, interesting! *Crottes de Recogne.* Aha! 'A necklace made of the fossilized genital attributes of a bear, found in a cave in the little Belgian town of Recogne at the end of the 19th century. Scientists have dated this curious adornment to the beginning of the Christian era. According to the more widely-held hypothesis, it is a precursor of the modern rosary, and evidence of a very early evangelisation in this area.' What strange places research takes you to!

But, dear reader, I have indulged your patience too long! To the point! *Crottes de Recogne* are a kind of Belgian charcuterie which hail, quite simply, from the village of Recogne. And they come in the shape of little round sausages joined to one another in a string. They are a typical savoury product of the Ardennes, like the long, thin sausages called *Pipes d'Ardenne:* they are very dry, extremely salty and hard enough to remove all the milk teeth of any local child in the first year of primary school.

So why are they called *'Crottes de Recogne'?* I heard this on the radio. Once upon a time in Recogne, there lived an ogre who, like all ogres, suffered from warts on his nose and ate little children. This evil soul hid in an underground lair that consisted of several interconnected caves. Written evidence of this story has been found in the parish records from September 1823, and the same author

© belgiumtheplaceto.be TM - J Jeanmart

of those lines was responsible for the creation of the term *Crotte de Recogne,* because he relied on the words of some villager, who was unable to pronounce the letter g. So instead of *grotte* (cave) he wrote *crotte…*

Unfortunately, I never got to the end of this story, as a sudden attack of hunger made me abandon my radio to head for the larder in the next room. And then I thought: what on earth is this all about? Just look at the things. There is no linguistic mystery here, just straightforward observation and a touch of earthy Ardennes humour.

L' Avisance

Qu'est-c'qui ça po one avisance? That's Walloon, the local language of southern Belgium, aka Wallonia. It's a version of French, if you like, and like many subsidiary languages that are kept alive primarily through speech, it doesn't have an official written form, and spellings are left to the whim of editors or to whoever is transliterating it. Despite the not-so-colossal scale of our kingdom, the language differs considerably according to where you are looking: Tournai, Liège, Charleroi, Mons, Bastogne, Verviers, Petit-Rechain, Montbliart, Torgny, you name it. Basically, get out your detailed map of Belgium and list everything that appears to the south of the Potato Curtain that divides Wallonia from Flanders.

The vocabulary used in the West is more *picard,* which spills over into France (viz. the region called Picardy), while that of the east is more Germanic. Hence the Walloon of the centre could be said to be more pure, but that's an assertion that I'll keep to myself, for fear of alienating a large portion of the potential clientele of this masterpiece.

So, the phrase at the top of this article means more or less: What's that strange thing? And indeed, this sausage wrapped in puff pastry is, without doubt, a strange thing, but it is an authentic speciality of the town of Namur. I have never seen the user manual, but I believe that it is just as good hot, warm or cold, with or without mustard. In my opinion, hot is perfection. But who am I to dictate the best way to eat an *avisance?*

© belgiumtheplaceto.be TM - J Jeanmart

Namur © belgiumtheplaceto.be TM - J Jeanmart

The Reinhardstein castle in Ovifat, in the valley of the Warche.
Province of Liège ©WBT - S. Wittenbol

5. Specialities of the Province of Liège:

The city Liège and its province – open recipient to the cultures of the north, west and south of Europe across all time – is a destination known for a wide variety of reasons by the British.

There is, of course the history: modern, first and foremost, and the heroic resistance of Liège and its forts, and its stubborn and tenacious citizens, during the two World Wars. More romantic: Spa, the town of celebrated mineral springs which blossomed as an élite watering hole in the 19th century, and which has given its name to all other spas, to the point where the world no longer connects the word to the place.

Trivia point: Huy, on the River Meuse, was the first town to the north of the Alps to benefit from a charter of liberty, granted by its lord to its burghers in 1066. English readers will recognize that date: as it happens, the mother of William the Conqueror, Arlette (or Herleva) was born in Huy, at least according to the Hutois (as the people of Huy are known), and they have raised a statue to her in her memory.

The Province of Liège has plenty of other famous progeny, of wide and varied accomplishment. The 8th and 9th-century Carolingian kings Charles Martel, Pepin the Short and Emperor Charlemagne were all born in Liège territory. The electrical engineer Zénobe Gramme was born in Amay. Rennequin Sualem, whose ingenious machine at Marly supplied the water for the gardens and fountains of Versailles, was born in Jemeppe-sur-Meuse. The composers André Modeste Grétry and César Franck and the violinist and composer Eugène Ysaÿe were all born in Liège, as was Georges Nagelmackers, founder of the Compagnie Internationale des Wagons-Lits and the Orient Express. But Liège's most famous son was Georges Simenon, crime-writer extraordinaire, creator of Inspector Maigret, author of some 350 novels.

Then there's the sport: Standard de Liège and its footballing heroes (Roger Claessen was Belgium's George Best of the 1960s and 1970s, and more recently, Marouane Fellaini); the cycling classics Liège–Bastogne–Liège and the Flèche Wallonne, and the Formula One Belgian Grand Prix at Spa-Francorchamps – are jewels in the province's glittering sporting crown.

The nickname of the city of Liège is 'La Cité Ardente' (The Fiery, or Hot-Blooded City). It owes that to the passionate adulation of the French poet and novelist Victor Hugo, who was fascinated by the power and the night-time spectacle of the blast furnaces of its steel industry. This lyrical flight of fancy was coined as homage to the economic lungs of the region, which exhaled its hot breath for nearly 150 years until the depletion of natural resources beneath the ground met with the emergence of more efficient and younger international competition after the Second World War. But the city still clings to the label, seeing 'La Cité Ardente' as an apt encapsulation of the Liégeois character.

Liège has had a separate history from the rest of the country. In contrast to the other provinces and to Brussels, Liège was never occupied by the Spanish, Austrians, Dutch or French until 1789. There have of course been conflicts and allegiances in the innumerable wars between the French and the Dutch, the Catholics and the Protestants, but these never amounted to more than that.

Liège was a Prince-Bishopric, with territory that extended well beyond the present limits of the Province to include Maastricht (now in the Netherlands), Tongres and Hasselt (now in the Flemish region of Belgium), as well as enclaves in the modern provinces of Namur (Dinant, Couvin) and Belgian Luxembourg (Bouillon, which Godefroy de Bouillon sold to the Prince-Bishops to finance the First Crusade). At the bottom line, to confront Liège meant engaging in a Holy War against the entire papal empire. This unusual status conferred upon the city of Liège an incredible concentration of religious institutions. Liège was said to be a paradise for priests, and hell for women (as practically all the men in Liège were priests) – to the point where, in the 12th century, there was not enough room in the convents. It was then that a preacher from Liège called Lambert le Bègue invented the famous pious but secular refuges for women called Béguinages – a movement that later spread to Flanders, the Netherlands and Germany.

The towers and spires of the churches, the basilica and the cathedral today are the last witnesses in the Liège skyline of this highly religious period. The 12th-century baptismal font of the collegiate church of St Barthélemy is a masterpiece of Mosan art (the distinctive art of the Meuse Valley), and is one of the Seven Wonders of Belgium, bearing witness to the high status of Liège during the eight centuries of rule by the Prince-Bishops. Today the city is more famous perhaps for having the largest pedestrianized zone in Europe, or for its huge outdoor staircase called the Montagne de Bueren leading up to the old Citadelle overlooking its bucolic Coteaux (hillsides) – the historic site of the vineyards and orchards of the religious institutions that lay at their feet. Liège also has several remarkable museums, including the Musée de la Vie Wallonne (Museum of Walloon Life, the best folk museum in the country) and the Musée Grand Curtius, with its world-class decorative arts collection.

This context has also generated a sense of identity, which is very strong and very old, on the part of the Liégeois themselves – who even had their own regiment, separate from that of the rest of the Belgians, in the French Revolutionary Army of the 1790s. That does not make the Liégeois insular; rather, although proud of belonging

© belgiumtheplaceto.be TM - J Jeanmart

to what they continue to call the Principality, they are welcoming, genial and self-deprecating. They'll say hello to a dog in a hat, as they say. All of which means that foreign visitors feel easily at home in Liège, and find it easy to blend in, whether they are just making a Sunday trip to La Batte, Europe's largest open-air market, or on a longer stay, for professional reasons or as a student.

While Liège (founded in the 4th century AD) can claim to be the oldest most northerly French-speaking city of Europe, the Liégeois have always kept up with what's going on in the world, witness its prowess in exports. Liège-born Louis de Geer is a splendid case in point: he introduced Walloon blast furnaces to Sweden in the 1620s, and is hailed as the father of the Swedish steel industry. Liège is blessed with an inalienably unique natural resource: its geographical location. It's just about impossible to go from north to south or from east to west in this part of the world without passing through Liège. It has the world's first international railway station, dating from 1843 when the Liège–Aachen link opened. Now this has been eye-catchingly upgraded with a superb and glittering new station designed by the Spanish-Catalan architect Santiago Calatrava.

The fruits of these long international trade links can be tasted in its cuisine, which is by far the richest and most varied of all the provinces of Belgium – to the extent that, to share the pages of this book evenly between provinces is not really representative. But you have to start somewhere.

Liège waffles –
les gaufres de Liège

What has always made me smile about Liège waffles – *les gaufres de Liège* – is that the people who sell them are often the very same as the ones who sell ice cream in summer. From the same vehicles. Some 30 years ago on the main square of Nivelles they were sold from a horse-drawn carriage.

An old horse and an old man. The waffles, the ice creams, his horse: that seemed to be his entire world. I used to buy a waffle from him from time to time. But sometimes I would be content simply to watch him, and to observe the world-weariness in the eyes of both man and horse. That soon slipped my mind as I jumped aboard my bus, laughing with my pals. Now that I've grown up, waffles are more a matter of a quick, sugar-intense snack, usually burning my lips, among a delirious crowd during an afternoon's shopping.

There are waffles, and there are waffles. *Gaufres de Liège* differ subtly from *gaufres de Bruxelles* (see page 22) and are more widely available; nicely caramelised, and made by a good ba<er, they rank among the greatest worldly delights. Particularly when you hit a big lump of pearl sugar that you can allow to melt slowly in your mouth.

THE BEST WAFFLES MAY BE YOUR OWN

750g plain flour, 270g warm milk, 70g fresh yeast, 3 whole eggs plus extra 2 yolks, 15g salt, ½ packet of vanilla sugar, 400g softened butter, 500g pearl or nib sugar

- Make the batter by mixing all the ingredients except the butter and the nib sugar. Cover with a cloth, and leave it to rise for 30 minutes.
- Knead the softened butter into the batter, then add the pearl sugar.

© belgiumtheplaceto.be TM - J Jeanmart

- Divide the batter into balls of 100g, and let them rest for 15 minutes.
- Grease a waffle-iron with pork fat, then heat it up on the stove; add the batter and cook on both sides for three minutes in total.

Le Lacquemant

When Bertha met Roger Lacquemant, she had no idea that she and he would achieve posterity as a result of a little flight of fancy. The modern form of *lacquemant* is a favourite treat for the Liégeois (the people of Liège) during their magnificent October Fair, or Foire de Liège. But – poignant paradox in Belgium's age-old Flemish–Walloon rivalry – *lacquemant* is also hailed as a speciality of Antwerp. Ain't that just the way? North and South, on both sides of the Potato Curtain that divides our nation, we love these sticky little delights. But back to the history. During the dark night of the ball at the October Fair (it dates back to the 12th century, an era of non-stop partying, I'll have you know) everyone was singing and feasting except poor Bertha and Roger Lacquemant.

The Lacquemants danced in silence; they weren't great talkers anyhow, those two. They weren't talking now because they were thinking of their new recipe: a super waffle cooked in less than three minutes. Bertha was thinking about the stalls that they would open all over town and across the country, across the world, selling these special waffles, coated with their magical splodge of goo. Roger Lacquemant, for his part, was thinking of how to get the recipe registered by law. History has retained his name by virtue of the 'Lacquemant laws'. They involved a complete revision of the traditional recipe for *gaufres de Liège* (see page 56). As they danced and said nothing, they were already savouring the happiness of the days ahead. This waffle would be fabulous: thick, rich, filled with and bathed in a syrup made of sugar, honey and orange blossom water. In the days when Europe was discovering the world and mad for things exotic, orange blossom was the ticket. But the syrup should be no more than warm, so as not to burn the consumers...

In short, what could possibly go wrong? They go back home.

The following day, Roger knocks out the batter, while Bertha heats up the waffle-iron. Now the batter has risen: it's the critical moment. He takes a portion of dough, rolls it, turns it, opens the iron and pops it in. Cooking now. The suspense is palpable.

The silence of anticipation. Open it up. Arggh! he exclaims. It's flat, or virtually flat – as flat as a tax return. But where is that syrup? Pour it all over it, everywhere. It's sticky, gleaming oilily in the dark night. It's far from clear that the thing will work at all! Roger is on the verge of tears. All those nights thinking this through with Bertha. And now nothing: more a flannel that a waffle.

It is at this moment that destiny comes knocking at the door. It's their apprentice, a child found among the reeds on the River Meuse, named Maurice Tchantchèsdinanesse in honour of the knockabout folk heroes of Liège, Tchantchès and his wife Nanesse. He sees the thing, and asks if he can taste it. With a weary nod of the head, Roger acquiesces. Surprise! Maurice is ecstatic! So ecstatic that he cries out with pleasure and the whole street comes running to see what the fuss is about.

That was one October a long, long time ago. Ever since then *lacquemants* are eaten every year in memory of this happy moment. Well, it's something like that anyhow – give or take a few of the details. Wikipedia tells us that *lacquemant* was invented by Désiré Smidts (a.k.a. Désiré de Lille) in 1903 while working for a company called Établissements Lacquemant in Antwerp before he moved to Liège, and it was later named after his former employer, Berthe (Bertha) Lacquemant. But you can't believe everything you read.

Tartes de Tancrémont

In 1940, the Fort de Tancrémont – one of a series of muscular fortresses built in the 1930s to defend the approaches to Liège – was distinguished by the obstinacy of its Commandant, and the courageous resistance of its soldiers, who only gave themselves up to their German aggressors the day after the rest of the Belgian Army had surrendered. Julius Caesar had declared that 'The Belgians are the bravest of the Gauls', and undoubtedly at Tancrémont there is something irreducibly Gaulish, which will forever resist an invader. And if this valiant Fort is today speckled with sheep grazing peacefully on the green pasture that covers it, it is clear that the spirit of Tancrémont will continue to be fêted long after the guns have been silenced.

The name also lives on through the marvellous, big tarts that the villagers have produced, generation after generation, to the pleasure of all the happy visitors who come to this hamlet from far and wide, and across borders, to satisfy their sweet-tooth cravings.

It's simple: the Bruxellois are mocked for their *tarte au riz* by the Liégeois, who have their own version; they are ridiculed in turn by the people of Verviers who claim to have invented it. But the ones who have the last word are the Tancrémontois: say *tarte au riz,* and many Belgians will say Tancrémont. But it doesn't stop there. Tancrémont is the Holy Grail for all lovers of fruit tarts: apricots, strawberries (strictly when in season), *myrtilles* (bilberries – a delight that will turn your teeth a very medieval colour, but quite simply irresistible).

The tarts are made in very large sizes: about 60 to 70 cm (24 to 28 inches) in diameter. But you don't have to organize a marriage or wait for a christening to enjoy one: the pâtisserie will sell you slices if you wish, permitting you to have fun creating a kind of circular

© belgiumtheplaceto.be TM - J Jeanmart

patchwork, memorable both for its looks and its wondrous variety of its flavours.

Tancrémont is a few kilometres from the celebrated Marian shrine at Banneux, where the Virgin Mary appeared to a girl in 1933 and revealed a healing spring. So it is with a touch of humour, perhaps, that my favourite pâtisserie has chosen to call itself Péché Mignon (literally, Little Sin, or weakness). If you are in the neighbourhood of Spa (perhaps for a Formula One Grand Prix at the Spa-Francorchamps circuit), don't forget to make a little detour to Tancrémont; it's on the slope of a hill that has wonderful views all the way to Germany and the Netherlands – and your taste buds will be eternally grateful.

La Salade Liégeoise

Everything is a bit different in Liège. It's not just me who thinks so: the people of Liège – the "Valorous Liégeois", to use the epithet of a famous revolutionary, patriotic song – also proudly proclaim this difference themselves.

It's the same with *Salade liégeoise:* the city's most famous and beloved dish is hard to pin down. Every family has its own recipe, and each claims it has the edge and embodies its truest form. It appears that there are even distinct differences between versions north and south of the River Meuse, which slices through the city. It wouldn't surprise me if there was now a version associated with Santiago Calatrava's astonishing new Liège-Guillemins station as well. Usually, the chief variations depend upon whether or not one includes onions and frisée (curly endive) lettuce.

© belgiumtheplaceto.be TM - J Jeanmart

THE ESSENTIALS: FRENCH BEANS, POTATOES AND VINEGAR

For my version you need: 500g French beans *(haricots princesses),* 350g potatoes (see below), 125g lardons (smoked bacon pieces), 2 shallots, butter, 3 tbsp red wine vinegar, a frisée lettuce (optional).

- For perfection and the most delectable dish imaginable, use pink fir apple potatoes *(corne de gatte),* the queen of waxy potatoes, cooked in their skins.
- The French beans should be *al dente* and bright green (if overcooked, they go limp and grey). To achieve this, boil them to just-cooked in salted water, then tip them into a dish of cold water and ice-cubes.
- At the next stage you will normally start salivating. Don't forget to close your mouth and swallow.
- Fry the lardons and shallots in butter until they begin to brown, then deglaze the pan with the vinegar and reduce the liquid by half.
- Drain the French beans; warm them gently with the potatoes, cut into bite-sized chunks. Now add the lardons and shallots.
- Mix well together; gently fold in the frisée lettuce – if you are on that side of River Meuse.
- Warm vinegar and bacon – it's almost a sin.
- You could also provide *un boket d'lard et d'socisse* (a bit of bacon and sausage), and tie your napkin around your neck because, from the first, succulent forkful, things tend to start getting messy.

Kidneys à la Liégeoise – Les rognons à la liégeoise

Dear reader – you who are devouring this book with such ravenous appetite – I can only hope to intimate the exquisite scope of Liège gastronomy that ranges from *lacquemants* (see page 57) to their famous *boulets* (meatballs; see page 154) in sauce sweetened by the divine *Sirop de Liège* (see page 131). On the way, let's not forget the *rognons* (kidneys). *Rognons à la liégeoise* is a classic dish that is taught in all the best hotel-and-catering schools.

I feel this welling desire to tell you how to make *Rognons à la liégeoise* as it was done in the times of the Prince-Bishops of Liège, who ruled over the city and a large autonomous swathe of Belgium from 972 to 1794. This is the classic method, the best, the most astonishing, but one that, sadly, you very rarely find. So, listen up: be prepared to be amazed. You begin of course by cleaning the kidneys – calves' or veal kidneys, if you want to do it properly. Since the heyday of *Rognons à la liégeoise,* the dish was democratised and pig's kidneys have been permitted to infiltrate.

Kidney-cleaning is a gas: I know people who do it for a hobby. If I want to relax, I clean a few kidneys. Time and patience are prerequisites: strip off the outer membrane and surgically remove the white fatty bit in the middle. If you are a real cook, you'll set aside the fat to make pike quenelles. If not I don't know what you can do with it; perhaps soften the leather of your boy's football boots – who knows!

Cooking *Rognons à la liégeoise* begins in the kitchen, then continues in the dining room, where the Maître d'hôtel, armed with his frying pan, completes the business in front of their Majesties. He removes kidneys from the pan just as they begin to exude droplets of blood. The pan is deglazed and then flambéed with jenever gin – that would be *pékèt* in Liège (see page 137).

© belgiumtheplaceto.be TM - J Jeanmart

Add some veal stock and crushed juniper berries (essential!). Finish the sauce with a knob of butter to thicken it slightly. The kidneys are then cut into slices, arranged on the plates, and coated with sauce. There, in public. Such an affront to their modesty!

Well, you won't see it done like that these days, so you'll just have to try it in the privacy of your own home. And don't let that stop you ordering *Rognons à la liégeoise* in a restaurant and eating them with gusto; however they are prepared, it's a dish to savour.

© belgiumtheplaceto.be TM - J Jeanmart

Ardennes Landscape © belgiumtheplacetobe TM

6. Specialities of the Province of Belgian Luxembourg: Hardcore Ardenne!

The Province of Belgian Luxembourg has a reputation for being a bit dull, like the stereotypical view that the British hold of Belgium as a whole – and likewise it could not be more utterly misguided.

For one thing, covering much of the southernmost part of the country, it is very hilly. If you ever believed Belgium was flat, try crossing this part of it on a bicycle!

In every part of the province there are enchanting vistas – a match for just about anywhere in the world. It is the setting for many of the beautiful legends of this part of Europe. Straddling Celtic and Germanic traditions, fairies, goblins, elves, witches and knights are the denizens of its woods. And in our times these were the source of inspiration for the little blue creatures called the Smurfs (known as Schtroumpfs in Belgium), the worldwide phenomenon that came from the imagination of Peyo (the pen name of Pierre Culliford), who spent many holidays with his in-laws in the midst of the fabled and mysterious Anlier Forest.

Belgian Luxembourg occupies the greater part of the Belgian Ardennes range, (locally referred to as the Ardenne, without the s). This range is divided into two main areas: Gaumais in the far south and Ardennais (essentially the rest) – a distinction that has no obvious logic on the ground except to the local people concerned, but it's worth knowing about it.

Historically there was a Duchy of Luxembourg that embraced the Grand Duchy of Luxembourg (now a separate country) and the present Belgian Luxembourg. The meanderings of political and military history and the different languages spoken in these two parts have resulted in the division of the territory either side of the present border between Belgium and Luxembourg.

All Belgian children worthy of the name have spent at least a weekend in this magnificent province, especially if they have been a scout. The main places visited are Bouillon, with its impressive medieval castle; Durbuy, dubbed rather sweetly 'the world's smallest town', which actually relates to a town charter awarded in 1331; La Roche-en-Ardenne and its haunted fortress; and Bastogne and its memorial to the brutal Ardennes Offensive (the Battle of the Bulge) of 1944/45. These are the classic destinations. But what really makes Belgian Luxembourg special, and brings a unity to such diverse experiences, is the encounters with the local people. While they may be initially what the Belgians call *taiseux* (taciturn, reserved), when they warm to you they are firm friends for life.

Warm, but discreet: Tom Hanks was able to walk about in complete peace here when he was making the TV mini-series *Band of Brothers,* without a single paparazzo pointing a lens at him. Courageous (the harsh climate, a land that often proves difficult to tame, and an irrepressibly wild natural world have left their mark), stubborn, super-charming and truly generous, these are the traits of a character that have intimidated more than one – and including the most fearsome – of world conquerors.

Belgian Luxembourg possesses the most breathtaking landscape not only of all Belgium, but of all the Ardennes. The valley of the Semois, which twists and turns close to the border with France, offers the most unexpected panoramas, the most famous being the Tombeau du Géant (the Giant's Tomb) and the Saut des Sorcières (Witches' Leap). The pine forests beckon the hiker with promises of cool shade during summers that can sometimes be swelteringly hot. The deciduous forests provide a non-stop spectacle, lit by their unforgettable seasonal colours. But Belgian Luxembourg is not just a place for contemplative views: it also has facilities for a wide range of strenuous activity holidays, from hiking and kayaking to mountainbiking and rock climbing… to name but a few.

The symbol of the Belgian Luxembourgeois is a tusked and alert-looking wild boar, clearly with some intention on its mind. It illustrates well the Province's spirit of self-driven determination, closely in tune with what nature so generously provides. That is true too of their culinary traditions: nourishing, robust and richly redolent of their remarkable landscape.

© belgiumtheplaceto.be TM - J Jeanmart

Ardennes Delicatessen:

Saucisson d'Ardenne

In French there are two words for sausage: *saucisse and saucisson*. So what's the difference? A *saucisse* is made to be cooked, as the English do for breakfast (strange things happen when you are an island nation). A *saucisson* is sold ready to eat, and usually sliced (in other words, like salami). And that is what Saucisson d'Ardenne is. Actually, it's a by-product of the Jambon d'Ardenne business, made from minced off-cuts mixed with pork (and sometimes beef) and pork fat, plus various herbs and spices. The mixture is then stuffed into sausage skins and smoked over oak or beech wood, to create a very distinctive dry, smoky finish. Saucisson d'Ardenne comes in four shapes and sizes: *saucisson, petit saucisson, pipe* (literally, 'pipe', long and thin) and *collier* (literally, 'necklace', long enough to be made into a ring). Because of the smoking process, the shape has a pronounced effect on the taste.

Saucisson d'Ardenne comes from exactly the same region as Jambon d'Ardenne. It is, however, not yet similarly protected by an *Indication géographique protégée* (IPG) label. In the recent past, Flemish manufacturers of a similar product went to court to protect their right to continue to call it Saucisson d'Ardenne: this was taken up by the press as a typical Flanders vs Wallonia spat, and dubbed 'La Guerre du Saucisson' (The Sausage War). The mind boggles! Anyhow, in 2012 it was resolved by the Conseil d'État (the supreme administrative court in Belgium) in favour of the Ardennais. Hooray! In the continued absence of an IPG, members of the Association des Producteurs de Saucisson d'Ardenne nail their colours to the mast with labels such as *'Saucisson d'Ardenne authentique'*. Accept no substitute!

© WBT. Emmanuel Mathez

Pâté d'Ardenne

So here's the thing. The French word pâté comes from *pâté en croute,* which means 'in a pastry crust'. That's because, in olden days, that's how chopped meat preparations were made. They were also made in lidded earthenware cooking pots called *terrines,* which amounts to the same thing in terms of sealed-in flavour. So, after baking in the oven, and allowing to cool and rest a while so the meat juices form a delicious, enrobing jelly, the resulting meat product is called a terrine, or a pâté. These days 'pâté' tends to indicate a smoother, more milled and spreadable product, while 'terrine' suggests something lumpier, served in slices.

Pâté d'Ardenne has become a bit of a generic title for a fairly rough kind of pâté; it might equally be labelled *pâté de campagne* – basic country pâté. Which it is not to say it isn't good, especially if you are buying pâté made by a real butcher, rather than the debased, industrialized stuff found in supermarkets. Pâté d'Ardenne is prepared from pork meat, pork liver (and maybe some chicken liver) and pork fat, in equal proportions, combined with chopped shallots, garlic, thyme, cloves, nutmeg, pepper, salt, cream, eggs and brandy. Some cooks will add slivers of cooked ham to the mix, too.
In Belgium, you serve this kind of pâté with gherkins. Always.

So what happened to the pastry crust? you ask. Has it been forgotten? Not in the Gaumais region in the far south of the Province of Luxembourg, it hasn't. Here, their famed *Pâté gaumais* is a proper, crusted meat pie, made with choice pieces of lean pork. Cut into cubes, the pork pieces are first marinaded for a couple of days in wine and vinegar, garlic, shallots, bayleaves and cloves, then baked in a round case of pasty at least 15cm (6 inches) across, and more usually twice that size. Eaten hot or cold, *Pâté gaumais* is so good that the European Union has awarded it official IGP status

© OPT - Emmanuel Mathez

(Indication géographique protégée), so other regions can't pinch the recipe and pass it off as their own. So you have to stop and buy some when you're in the Gaume: every butcher and baker does *Pâté gaumais,* sold with a little *hostie* (literally, communion wafer) in the middle, to verify that precious authenticity.

Jambon d'Ardenne

It is surely no accident that the French word *jambon* (ham) contains the word *bon* (good). It is probably one of the factors that our legislators took into consideration when giving *Jambon d'Ardenne* an IGP *(Indication géographique protégée)*, which prevents the use of the name except by authentic producers in the Ardennes. *Beurre d'Ardenne* (Ardennes butter) and *Pâté Gaumais* (pâté of the Gaume region in Belgian Luxembourg) are similarly protected. The fame of *Jambon d'Ardenne* has spread well beyond our borders, much to the delight of those friendly Ardennais farming folk who can become just as swollen with pride – *dikke nek* or 'fat necked' as the Bruxellois would say – as the French about such things. As in some quarters such a suggestion might cause offence, I should perhaps stress that I'm just poking friendly fun here. The French *Jambon sec des Ardennes* (like the English, the French add an s to their part of the region) is similarly protected under an IGP of its own, so if you want to compare the levels of pride, the evidence is there to be collected.

Jambon d'Ardenne lives exclusively in the Belgian province of Luxembourg, although it can sometimes wander into neighbouring cantons in the provinces of Liège and Namur. It is a dried-cured meat, made from a whole leg. The leg is salted, either by rubbing salt in, or by immersing it in brine. Contrary to widely held misapprehensions in the rest of Belgium outside the natural habitat of *Jambon d'Ardenne,* smoking is optional. When it is smoked (no, don't try rolling up a slice to do this, you won't be able to light it), it is done with wood or sawdust from rigorously selected timber. Such rigour relates to an admirable insistence on natural processes. Salting and smoking a leg of pork anywhere outside the Belgian Ardennes simply does not yield the same flavour: it lacks the microclimate of the Ardennes and the seasonal qualities of

© belgiumtheplaceto.be TM - J Jeanmart

temperature, humidity, and the circulation of damp, fresh air which are indispensable for the processes of maturing and drying.

I will end this sermon on *Jambon d'Ardenne* with some consumer advice. Watch out for counterfeits! Like all products basking in a fully justified renown, it has been unscrupulously imitated by numerous producers of cured meats, who will sell you four slices of common or garden smoked ham under the guise of *Jambon d'Ardenne.* Pre-packaged products in plastic containers with the semblance of a natural product and a sprig of parsley printed on the packaging to make it look pretty are – for the most part – 'smoked' by spraying on a kind of syrup and leaving it for 24 hours. So, beware! Any Belgian who makes this mistake risks a rap over the knuckles when Mother sets out the dishes.

Maitrank

Before I engage you on the subject of *Asperula odorata* (no, it's not a new brand of domestic cleaning agent), I have to tell you a funny thing. Once, when browsing the official website for Maitrank – the drink that's the speciality of the town of Arlon – I came upon a recipe for *Choucroute au Maitrank* (sauerkraut, or pickled cabbage, made with Maitrank). Clearly with Maitrank, the sky's the limit! You can bung it in every sauce in sight – sauce to accompany chicken, rabbit, pigeon… you get the drift. In fact, just about everything edible around these parts should be given a dose of Maitrank, no questions asked. OK, it's true, I haven't yet seen a recipe for Buitoni tinned *Ravioli au Maitrank.*

So what is this stuff? It's the 'May drink', according to the name. It involves the maceration of a little perfumed plant, *Asperula odorata* or woodruff, which grows beneath the beech trees of this beautiful region. It didn't grab the attention of the Druids who were drawn to the mistletoe that grows in the upper boughs, but it excited great interest among the Arlonnais, who, as is well known, are a fun-loving lot. So, following an ancestral recipe, the woodruff is steeped in Moselle wine, sliced oranges and a number of other semi-secret ingredients, then filtered to produce this agreeable drink.

The origin of Maitrank dates back at least a thousand years, and to Germany, where the monks of the Abbey of Prüm had the habit of steeping woodruff in the wine that they drank in spring to fortify themselves after the rigours of winter. A fine habit which I can thoroughly recommend.

The last weekend of May, in Arlon, is the Fête du Maitrank – just the moment to blow away the last of the winter cobwebs with a time-honoured remedy.

© WBT. Emmanuel Mathez

L' Orval

OK now, listen up. There are six Trappist beers in Belgium. Heavenly beers, made by Cistercian monks who have taken a vow of strict observance (if not complete silence), or by lay brewers under their careful supervision. Three of the beers are connected to monasteries in Flanders: Westmalle, Westvleteren and Achel. And three are in Wallonia: Rochefort, Chimay and Orval.

Monasteries have been brewing beer since the Middle Ages, and the Trappists since the 17th century. But here's a strange phenomenon that I have discovered while researching this book: things that I had imagined to be integral and inseparable parts of the Belgian identity since the dawn of time are sometimes, at most, only a few decades old. And Orval beer is one such: it came into being only in the 1930s. True, there was a previous incarnation. At the height of the abbey's luminous splendour, sometime in the Middle Ages, brewing was carried out here. But the French Revolution and its trail of destruction put a stop to that, and the abbey, 1793.

The magnificent renovation of the abbey at the start of the 20th century called for huge funds, and beer provided a source of revenue. It was a layman of German origins who recreated Orval beer, using a process that was fashionable in England at the time. Hence this magnificent beer is as much a product of Europe as of Belgium: created by a German, made in Belgium using Czech hops, following a process that is partly English.

Orval is also characterised by its superb, skittle-shaped bottle, unchanged for at least as long as my memory of it. Like every Belgian beer, it also has its own tailor-made glass which supposedly brings out its best qualities; in my view though, Orval's open, chalice-like glass fails to do full justice to the beer's soft fragrance.

© belgiumtheplaceto.be TM - J Jeanmart

The label recalls its origins in the 1930s, but the image refers to the legend that the Abbaye Notre Dame d'Orval was founded in the 11th century by Countess Matilda of Tuscany after a trout miraculously recovered her wedding ring, which she had lost in a local spring. A wondrous tale to match the complexity of the beer itself, especially after a several years in the cellar.

© Orval OPT - Flemal

7. Food for Gourmets

© belgiumtheplaceto.be TM - J Jeanmart

Steak tartare, the Belgian way – *le filet américain*

Here's the type of dish that people develop a real passion for, as much to write about it as to eat it. But first the big question: why do we Belgians say *filet américain* (literally, American fillet) when referring to this dish of raw ground beef, while the rest of the world says *steak tartare?* No American eats raw meat like this, surely? So where does the name spring from? According to various websites, Charleroi was the place, perhaps reflecting its sister city of the same name in Pennsylvania, founded in 1890. Or the Flemish town of Vilvoorde, northeast of Brussels.

Now there's a thought. Until a few decades ago, Vilvoorde was the site of the biggest horse abattoir in the country. And to begin with *américain* was made of horse meat: ah, yes – it was, if you like, the elephant in the room. It was perhaps because of the horse meat that it got labelled *américain:* cowboys, Indians, the cavalry that always arrived too late – they all got about on horses. At the start of the 20th century, at the dawn of cinema, people were quick to make the link. Well, that's a plausible theory. And while we're at it, here's another question: for some years now, and more and more frequently, you come across a variant of the *sandwich américain* called Martino, composed of *filet américain,* mustard, ketchup and a touch of Tabasco. It's nothing to write home about. But who is Martino? Why Martino? Who knows. You might as well ask why cows have horns and not horses. Enough with the questions!

So *filet américain* is basically finely ground beef. It can be dressed up in various ways, according to taste. Worcestershire sauce is often in the frame. Chopped onions and capers are other options. However, the raw yoke of an egg presented in its half shell in the middle of the meat, as some restaurants insist, has little to recommend it. Butchers do *américain préparé,* with their own ready-mix of ingredients. But for me, straight and unadorned *américain non-préparé,* served with salt, pepper, and a dollop – or *une clouche,* if you want to say it like a true Belgian – of mayonnaise… well, that's really the picture of perfection. Especially if accompanied by chips (and mayonnaise).

The White Lady – *la dame blanche*

The ubiquitous dessert called *Dame Blanche* (White Lady) first appeared in Belgium in the wake of the big match that pitted the Belgian film star Jean-Claude Van Damme ('The Muscles from Brussels') against world chess grandmaster Bobby Fischer, and which saw the American triumph in 2 minutes 30 seconds after his famous opening with the White Queen (*Dame Blanche* in French). Ah yes, our actor opted for black: bad decision! Now, big question: after that, how are you going to believe anything I say?

Did *Dame Blanche* really appear in Belgium at a given moment, or has it been part of out food culture for ever? I would tend towards the second proposition because in fact no one knows the origins of this famous dessert. So feel free to create your own fantasy. You've heard mine.

What is known for sure is that *Dame Blanche* is the first choice of desserts for mass catering, for children, and – it should be said – for some gastronomes. Making it is essentially very simple, but you have to insist on good ingredients, and you need a certain knack. Sadly, this is all too often overlooked. A 5-litre container of La Fermette ice cream from the supermarket, whipped cream that's been standing around for three days, and a giant tub of chocolate sauce may be all you need to win over a group of school kids on a coach trip to Brussels after their deep-fried frozen *croquettes aux crevettes* and a *carbonnade flamande* (beef stew cooked in beer), but if you're old enough to know better, you should stand your ground and refuse to have anything to do with it.

IT'S BEEN A PART OF OUR FOOD CULTURE FOR EVER

- For a good *Dame Blanche*, you need top-quality, hand-made vanilla ice cream, a chocolate sauce made from good dark Belgian chocolate slowly melted in a bain-marie.

© belgiumtheplaceto.be TM - J Jeanmart

- Mix the chocolate with a little milk to prevent it from coagulating on the ice cream like a cheap marshmallow cake, and fresh cream that has been beaten to slightly sub-Chantilly froth.
- And don't forget you'll need a Pirouline biscuit – a rolled, chocolate-lined wafer– to crown the whole edifice.

Brown shrimp croquettes – *Les croquettes de crevettes*

Brown shrimps, or *crevettes grises* (see page 78), are an integral part of our national gastronomic culture, and – in contrast to mussels – are a product from our very own shores, albeit not always. They famously appear in the guise of a croquette, the celebrated *croquette aux crevettes;* however, it's in these circumstances that the foreign spies in our midst have to be unmasked. Ah yes, when you are not Belgian, you will just cut into a *croquette aux crevettes* and tuck in without hesitation, even at the risk of burning your tongue and palate (and burning yourself a second time when you try to spit it out). Croquettes have their cult following and their masters, but can also be the source of disappointment and shame.

But to cut into a *croquette aux crevettes* at Aux Armes de Bruxelles, a celebrated restaurant in the heart of Brussels… Now this is really a moment of joy. After this, apart from your own, by which I mean those you have prepared yourself at home – after this, nothing will quite match the experience. When you are served a sluggish *croquette,* accompanied by three scrawny sprigs of parsley fried to a carbonised crisp, you will dream, with a sob rising in your throat, of those perfect croquettes. You will dream of their beautifully crunchy casing that is not overegged with breadcrumbs. You will dream of their filling that is perfectly soft and moist without being runny. You will dream of the shrimps in serried ranks, readied for devouring. You will also recall the bush of fried fresh parsley that accompanied it. What more can you say? In the name of *croquettes aux crevettes* many crimes have been committed which have so far gone unpunished.

© belgiumtheplaceto.be TM - J Jeanmart

Peaches with tuna – *la pêche au thon*

Now here's a dish that divides the nation. *Pêche au thon.* It is fantastically simple, something you can rustle up in your kitchen in two seconds flat. Open a tin of peach halves in syrup; drain. Open a tin of tuna, drain, mix with mayonnaise, pepper. Place a scoop of the fish in a peach half, and sprinkle with paprika and parsley or chives if you are being fancy. Devour. Or not. Let's face it: peaches and tuna fish – it's not going to be everybody's cup of tea. But those who love it, really love it. And everything is worth trying. Once.

Now, a word about the tuna. In most cases, it comes in a form that is not at all flattering: flesh pickled in brine, cooked and coated with olive oil, sitting in a round tin from which it takes its shape and, you might say, its colour. Well, before encountering this tragic fate, the tuna was a living being, with a touch of the superb about it. This proud animal is something of an adventurer, moving in schools from the Azores to the Bay of Biscay, from the Tropics to the Mediterranean. Whether it's a skipjack of 25 kg, or an albacore of 60 kg or an Atlantic bluefin tuna weighing several hundred kilos, this king of the sea never leaves its school. I recently heard about a school of tuna spotted one ordinary evening off Knokke-Heist on the Belgian coast: magic on "our" shores.

So your tins of tuna have been on quite a few adventures before ending up in your larder. Just a thought, as you reach for the tin opener. Easy dish, but complex getting there. And rapacious tuna fishing – with giant seine nets at least 1.6 km long, hauled in by cables – divides the world just as *Pêche au thon* divides the nation. So where do you stand?

© belgiumtheplaceto.be TM - J Jeanmart

Salted butter –
le beurre salé

In Belgium, like most things, butter also divides along linguistic lines. It is different in the Flemish north and the Walloon south, make no bones about it! In the north, the butter is unsalted – unadulterated, if you will. In the south, it is salted. My family are southerners, and where my parents live we have been buying butter from the same farm for 20 years or more. One day when I had the job of collecting it, I ended up helping to make the stuff.

Jacques' mother – for it was she who made the butter – used the week's cream, which was stored in the cellar, at a constantly cool but not glacial temperature. Storing allows the cream to mature. This slow maturation has a major influence on the taste of the butter. It is churned on Mondays, if my memory serves me well, in a wooden churn standing in a room designated for this purpose. The addition of the correct amount of salt during this churning process is fundamental to its success. When I asked her about it, she said 'it goes something like this' and threw a few handfuls of salt to the butter mix. How much? That remains her secret. Then comes the last part of the process: shaping the butter into 125g blocks by hand, using a wooden mould.

This butter changes colour according to the seasons: in summer it is very yellow, in winter very white. Around here, the cows are fed on grass, grass and more grass. And beet cake. Not industrialised pellets or meal: it's a farm from another era perhaps, but they are quite right.

Because it is also left to mature for a few days, the butter is full of flavour – so much so that it disconcerts the townies. One day a few years back a customer at the restaurant called me over and told me that my butter was rancid. That can happen; surprising, but… well, I did not dispute it. I went to the fridge, took out another piece,

© belgiumtheplace-o.be TM - Eric Boschman

cut it in two, tasted it and took the other half to the table. Three minutes later, the same zozo called me back and repeated that my butter was off. I explained to him that I had just tasted it, that it was perfectly fresh, and asked him what he did not like about it. And he patronisingly explained to me that it was because 'it had a taste'. Poor chap, poor things we all are, to prefer tasteless butter in plastic dishes or coated foil to full-flavoured farm butter.

The butter from my village does not fall within the *Appellation d'Origine Protegée* (AOP) of *'Beurre d'Ardenne,'* but it is almost as good. I thought of giving you the address of Jacques' and his mother's farm: it is on the left of the road that twists and turns as it mounts the long hill as one leaves the village in the direction of Sivry. But I won't say more than that. You'll find it, or somewhere like it, if you really want to, because the countryside is still, thankfully, peopled by the likes of Jacques. Don't forget them, because all the while rules full of good intentions, be they from the EU or regional governments, are trying to sanitize production. Technocrats want everything clean and shiny: forget taste, individuality, history. History is the enemy for both technocrats and sales. But a product that comes from a certain place, with a specific flavour, can't be sold like a bar of soap.

La tête de veau en tortue

In a cuisine as rich and celebrated as ours, it's perhaps a bit odd to find quite so many dishes involving tripe and offal – including this one and *choesels* (see page 19) – especially given that there are hardly any tripe butchers worthy of the name left in the kingdom.

You may know *tête de veau* (calf's head rendered into a form of charcuterie), but have you come across this version *'en tortue'*? Literally, that's 'in a turtle'. Why? Simply because the Madeira-enriched sauce traditionally poured over *tête de veau* was originally also used in the preparation of various types of turtle. Yes, they did that in the past.

In contrast to the *tête de veau* that we know today (which can still be very good), the original *tête de veau* was a luxury dish – the stuff of feasts. There were countless garnishes: brains, slices of truffle, shrimps, fried croutons. Just listing them puts one in mind of *Babette's Feast*.

This is true cooking, something that really takes time to prepare – not the flash-in-the pan creation of some TV chef. *Tête de veau en tortue* is, of course, not a name protected by law, but it is quite wrong to think that anyone can make it to a traditional recipe on a commercial basis. Once a grand dish prepared for big occasions, over time it became a classic of home cooking. Today it can be eaten hot or cold, both equally good. Personally, I tend to prefer it cold, cut into large cubes, to give it some body and some bite, and accompanied by a *sauce ravigote* – a vinaigrette-style sauce with mustard, chopped shallots, capers, and herbs etc. Or else in fine slices with a touch of *moutarde de Gand* (Ghent mustard).

To use that peculiar French expression, *'C'est vachement bon'*: it's really (literally, 'cowly') good!

© belgiumtheplaceto.be TM - J Jeanmart

Brown shrimps –
les crevettes grises

'Brown shrimps' is sometimes the translation. Simply 'shrimps' might do, but would that bring to mind the tiny brown shrimps of the North Sea, so beloved in Belgium, fiddly to peel and prepare but without parallel for flavour? In Belgium they are fished off the coast by night, cooked on board the boat without any preservative, chilled with a scattering of sea salt to fix their colour, and sold unpeeled in the morning markets. They are a gourmet's delight, but you have to seek them out among specialist fishmongers and restaurants, or buy them from fishermen on the coast. They have a very short shelf life: eat within two days of purchase.

If you really want the best, you have to get to know the shrimp fishermen and buy them alive, so you can cook them yourself in a court-bouillon (a light, aromatic stock of herbs and vegetables), then lay them out to cool on a marble slab, sprinkled with sea salt.

A bowl of *crevette grises*, with their skins and moustaches intact, peeled casually and eaten with a bit of the shell still *in situ* (they are that fiddly, and really it does not matter), to be accompanied by a glass of chilled white wine – what really could be better?

The Belgians have also discovered their magical affinity to tomato, to which we have dedicated an article of its own: *Tomates crevettes* (see page 18). And, of course, if you're lucky they will they feature in the classic Belgian dish *Croquettes aux crevettes* (see page 18.)

© belgiumtheplaceto.be TM - J Jeanmart

Gourmet grills

There are various models and variations on the theme, but a gourmet grill – also known as an *appareil à raclette* – is essentially a mini, tabletop, electric stove composed of two cooking levels separated by a heating element. This notorious element demands the use of oven gloves should you decide to eschew the lifting handles designed for this purpose, or prefer to take the even-more-foolhardy course of placing your fingers directly on the burning-hot metal. We can only then recommend either holding your burnt fingers in cold water, or placing the grill under cold water in order to detach the bits of oven glove which will have got stuck on the much-maligned element, which will have been guilty of nothing more than proving the rule.

The upper level consists of a cooking surface, or *plaque de chauffe* – also called the *'tour de chauffe'* (warm-up lap) by the little jokers who like to put all the mini sausages in a double ring around the edge of the said cooking surface, and make engine noises throughout the meal. This cooking surface in itself constitutes a serious danger. In addition to the risk of burning skin described above, there is also that posed by hot spitting fat. This cooking surface should be very lightly brushed with oiled while still cold. Repeat: lightly. Don't tip a bottle over it.

After switching on, by means of a cable plugged into a wall socket, the feast can begin. Meats, fish, vegetables… I could go on and on, as you might imagine! And more, as the lower level is equipped with dainty little dishes designed to hold pieces of *raclette* cheese, whose main property is to melt, then bubble, then stick to the element above, and then to the roof of your mouth. And if it is still burning hot at that point, oh joy! In general the meal passes off pretty well, and lasts a good hour, with happy faces all around the

© belgiumtheplaceto.be TM - J Jeanmart

table. At the end of it all, when you emerge triumphant, you feel a bit like the soccer team that has won promotion and will sing all the way back to the changing room. Ah, it's a wonderful life.

8. Junkily delicious

Les frites

How to you get 18 Belgians into a Citroën Deux-Chevaux? You throw a chip into it. You want more? Well, you're not going to get any more. I've had a sense-of-humour failure: it happens – particular over these tiresome 'Belgian jokes' that casually poke fun at our nation. But I made the exception above because there is an anthropological truth to the joke. Belgians do love their *frites*. (Chips, French fries, call them what you will in English. For the sake of transatlantic peace and goodwill, I'm going to stick to what we French-speaking Belgians call them.)

First, to the history of the *frite*. Who invented it? This is the subject of considerable controversy, but I can tell you the answer. It was the Belgians, of course. And more precisely, the Walloons. In the early 17th century, people on the banks of the River Meuse, at Huy, Namur, and Dinant, used to deep-fry little fish as a tasty snack. Then they found that potatoes, cut to about the same size, were also brilliant. The first fish and chips!

Let's take things step by step.

1. What exactly is a *frite?*
2. What makes a good *frite?*
3. When do you eat *frites?*
4. At what age can you start?

1. A *frite* is the child of the potato, a tuber brought back from the Americas by the Spanish conquistadors, and no doubt everyone enjoyed the cruise all the more for it. To be more precise, it is what in geometry is called a rectangular parallelepiped (or 3D rhomboid to its friends) with a square cross-section, extracted from a potato that is not too big, and not too small. A good *frite* will be golden and crisp – or what we call onomatopoeically *croustillante.*

2. A good raw *frite* should be regular in shape, and washed several times in water, or ideally soaked in water for half an hour before being dabbed and dried in a clean tea towel. But the biggest secret of the unquestioned superiority of the Belgian *frite* lies in – wait for it, drum roll – double-frying. The oil in all the best *friteries* or *fritkots* (the streetside stalls selling frites) in Belgium is 100% beef fat, called *blanc de boeuf.* You simply cannot get the desired degree of *croustillante*-ness any other way. (Sorry vegetarians!) First deep-fry the *frites* for 6–7 minutes at 160°C. Allow to drain and cool for 10 minutes, then cook them a second time at 175°C, until the frites are just so.

3. Generally in the second half of the day, from around lunchtime onwards. But there is no law against tucking in from first light.

4. In Belgium, from birth.

Sauces for frites

So, you've got your *frites* and, as you know, because they're Belgian, they are whatever chips should be: hot, golden, *croustillantes* – or at least they darned-well should be. So now, next thing: what sauce? What, from among the multi-coloured array of sauces on show at the *fritkot*, and the list as long as your arm, are you going to choose? Really: most *fritkots* list about 15!

Well, if you are a beginner, or indeed a seasoned traditionalist, there is really no difficulty. Mayonnaise, of course. That's the Belgian way. Nice, smooth, tasty egg-based mayonnaise is the perfect foil for the hot fat and sweet-dry carbohydrate of freshly fried *frites*. Trouble is, if you make your own mayonnaise (as you should, it isn't difficult, just oil and egg yolks and lemon and mustard whisked up together), the stuff you'll find at the *fritkot* won't quite be up to your standards. But, let's face it, that's going to be case whatever sauce you choose: we're talking *frites* in the street here – you're not exactly eating at the multi-starred 'Comme Chez Soi'!

So here's another dozen sauces for you to consider, described in rather idealized terms before industrial food-scientists do their work. And in alphabetical order, so I don't get a accused of favouritism:

Aioli Crushed garlic in a mayonnaise-style base.

Americaine Mayonnaise with chopped chervil, onion, celery, capers, cayenne pepper, white wine and brandy (apparently the Americans eat something like this with their lobster).

Andalouse The Spanish touch and the most popular one in Belgium: mayonnaise plus tomatoes, garlic, shallots, red and green peppers and a touch of chilli.

Béarnaise A classic sauce, which is a Hollandaise sauce (egg yolk, butter, lemon juice or white wine) with added shallots, chervil and tarragon.

BBQ Onions, sugar, ketchup, vinegar, mustard, cooked up together.

Cocktail Mayonnaise mixed with ketchup, with Worcestershire sauce and whisky – or another alcohol with a bit of an edge.

Curry Curry powder cooked into a sweetened béchamel sauce; or a curry-flavoured mayonnaise.

Ketchup Well, you know that one. The Belgians like it rather vinegary. Sometimes seen as 'curry ketchup'.

Mammouth Mayonnaise with tomato, onion, garlic and soy sauce, plus a bit of hot spice.

Pickles belges A kind of piccalilli – a sweet-sour, mustard-based condiment with crunchy chopped garden vegetables, ginger and tumeric. It's an old-school *sauce à frites,* rarely seen these days – more's the pity.

Pili-pili A hot chilli sauce.

Samouraï Mayonnaise mixed with ketchup, and spicy heat provided by *sambal oelek* (Indonesian chilli sauce) or North African *harissa.*

Tartare A mayonnaise with chopped capers, gherkins, and fresh green herbs (chervil, chives, tarragon, parsley).

The Machine gun – la mitraillette

The Belgian gastronomic arsenal contains not just *pistolets* (see page 128), but also *mitraillettes* – machine guns. And as a rough calculation, a *mitraillette* is the equivalent of 4–5 *pistolets*. Basically, it's a question of fire power.

You might come across a *mitraillette* at any large *friterie* or *fritkot* (streetside purveyor of *frites*/chips/fries), on either side of the linguistic Potato Curtain that divides our nation. Why *'mitraillette'*? In my humble opinion, and without researching this on Google, it's because of all the golden *frites* that tumble out of the *baguette*, cartridge-like. Perhaps there'll be some among you who have no idea what I'm talking about. Please refer to the picture that accompanies this text. See? It's half a baguette, sliced open and stuffed with *frites*. That's only the basics. But we won't be satisfied with that.

We also need meat. Hamburger, ham, cheese, *américain* (raw ground beef), and let's not forget the salad of *crudités* (raw chopped vegetables), and the mayonnaise. *Mitraillette:* it's a complete meal in itself.

It's a snack for a 30-strong commando unit back from a mission – and even then I don't know if they'll manage to eat it all. Yes, of course, I'm exaggerating, but only a little. A *mitraillette* is truly colossal. It's no laughing matter; this is a seriously big deal, and only the toughest of the tough need apply.

© Cedric Sophie

Le Cervelas

Le cervelas: 'a combination of meats of indeterminate origin compressed into the shape of a zeppelin.' Definition found by happy coincidence on the Web.

I think that Belgium will always have some kind of vaguely smoked doodahs placed on shiny counters to tempt workers clutching their glass of pils as they wait. Wait for their bus or train, wait for the working day to finish, wait for a discussion about the latest soccer game, wait for one last game of billiards before heading home.

Where there is beer, a smiling barmaid, a TV providing a constant background, there will be *cervelas.* Cut into thick slices with a splodge of mustard in the middle of the plate. The sausage skin cracks in your mouth, and the mustard stings. Just the ticket to take the edge off your hunger. Before heading off.

A *cervelas* in one hand, a hot cornet of *frites* burning the fingers of the other, your breath misting in the cold, coat collar turned up.

A *cervelas* at home, plain and simple, with an apéritif or just because you feel like it.

© belgiumtheplaceto.be TM - J Jeanmart

Spaghettis bolognaise

Even if Bologna is not exactly in the heart of Belgium, and even if our version of *spaghetti bolognese* bears little resemblance to the dish made in that city, it is a thread that runs through our lives, week after week, like our morning cups of coffee and *pistolet* buns every Sunday.

If you imagine an average Belgian of about 40 years of age, you can calculate – on the basis of one a week, minimum – that he or she will have eaten at least 2000 *spaghettis bolognaise*. I am not exaggerating, and while it is true one eats relatively few before the age of one, this lost year is soon recovered. Equipped with perhaps no more than six teeth, young Belgians in their high chairs will already be wielding their plastic spoons to tuck into spaghetti cut into small pieces by their attentive mothers.

It's found on children's menus in countless restaurants, catering for those that don't want fish fingers or chicken nuggets. During childhood or adolescence, we revel in home-cooked spaghetti, made with a tinned sauce to which ground beef has been added and left to simmer for the whole afternoon on the stove. During our years of studying, or in the early days of emancipation, the situation deteriorates: tinned sauce is all that's used, and what's more, the cheapest possible. The spaghetti is cooked in a 10-litre pan for at least 15 people, and ends up as a clump of pasta that has to be cut up with a saw. Often you don't even need to drain the spaghetti because all the water vanished four minutes into the cooking. Once embarked on their blossoming life as a couple and then as a family, Belgians return to the true path, that of the simmered sauce. The ingredients vary. Sometimes just plain tomato, sometimes a touch of fantasy is provided by mushrooms, peppers or carrots. The grated cheese may be Italian or otherwise. Who cares?

© belgiumthepaceto.be TM - J Jeanmart

Spaghettis bolognaise, not content to play their role at family meals, also makes an appearance as a lunchtime dish in bars and cafés, to be wolfed down with a glass of red house wine. You might think of it as a little snack to ease a burning hunger, but this can be a mistake as *Spaghettis bolognaise* is not something to be taken lightly. Well made, it can be a beautiful thing – and that's certainly the case with the ones I'm thinking of right now.

© belgiumtheplaceto.be TM - J Jeanmart

9. Sweet tooth

Filled chocolates – les pralines

Yes, Madame Van Pee, your little terrier has deposited a *praline* on my doormat. Luckily, Madame Van Pee is a local and knows what a *praline* is, in both senses of the word, thank goodness. But if she had been from France, for example, she might have wondered what I was on about.

For the purposes of this book, of course, we mean chocolates, or rather filled chocolates, known in Belgium as *pralines*. These marvels, the delight in which our tastebuds have luxuriated for a century now, owe their birth to a *chocolatier* of Swiss descent, one Jean Neuhaus. To the history of Belgium, we give our thanks! If we hadn't been so often invaded and so open to foreign influence, we might never have been so creative!

In 1912, this good Mr Neuhaus had the brilliant idea of pouring liquid chocolate into hollow moulds to create little shells just begging to be filled. To begin with he obliged with the mix of crushed hazelnuts and caramelised sugar known as *praliné*, hence the name adopted by Neuhaus for his creations. We also owe to Neuhaus, or rather to his wife, the invention of the *ballotin* – the neatly tapering cardboard box in which Belgian chocolates are sold. Before long, he and other chocolate manufacturers (Leonidas, Godiva and others) were filling their *pralines* with all kinds of other ingredients, flavours and textures – fruit pastes, liqueurs, marzipan, scented creams – founding the heritage that we bask in today.

Belgian *pralines* are generally pretty substantial. Weighing 15–18g, they are almost too big for a single mouthful. Unfortunately, most of us feel obliged to store them in the fridge, which is a catastrophe from the point of view of taste. Imagine a classic *praline* filled with fresh cream coming out of the cold. It's like biting into cold butter – a pretty mediocre sensation that falls far short of its potential.

For some years now, *praline*-makers and other *chocolatiers* have been exploring new avenues. Smaller chocolates, more original flavours, different shapes. Chocolate in Belgium is in a new stage of evolution. Welcome news indeed!

Les baisers de Malmedy

'Malmedy Kisses'. What a great name! I can't resist giving you the formula.

Take a trip to Malmedy, in eastern Belgium, one sunny day, visit the surrounding countryside, take a walk around the lake and dam at Robertville – it's always impressive. Then head for the centre of Malmedy. Switch off the engine. Get out of the car. Walk round to the passenger door. Lean in towards her mouth and kiss her deeply.

The same recipe works for the period of Malmedy's famous pre-lenten carnival, albeit that it's colder, and you can't park on the main square and your lips may be sore from the exertions of the Mardi Gras festivities. Alternatively, you could content yourself buying a *baiser de Malmedy* at a pâtisserie; less complicated, perhaps, and who knows, maybe almost as good.

Baisers de Malmedy have been around for a long time, and well before they were given this name, really. At the beginning of the 20th century they were referred to as *blankès meringues* (white meringues, as if there were any other kind). It would appear that it was their quality and more especially the local fresh cream which earned the things their new name: Kiss. Clearly passionate people these Malmédians; they could have settled for a handshake.

HOW TO MAKE A BAISER DE MALMEDY

- Bake two little meringues, the size of a coffee spoon.
- Allow to cool and dry. Fill with whipped cream. Open mouth.

© belgiumtheplaceto.be TM - J Jeanmart

La Cougnolle

The *cougnolle* (also called *cougnou*) has a large place in our hearts. At Christmas time, along with *spéculoos* in the shape of Saint-Nicolas, marzipan, mandarines, *nic-nac* biscuits (in the shapes of letters) sprinkled with icing sugar, *cougnolles* (and I prefer to speak about them as such, as my childhood unfurled in the land of *cougnolles,* not *cougnous*), these bizarre little 'bread of Jesus' cakes shaped like the baby Jesus, are among the few sweet treats that my parents and grandparents ever knew. We, the generation of the 1960s, had the luxury of knowing sweets of every colour, flavour and shape, but nonetheless *cougnolles* were a key feature of the happiness that we won't ever forget.

As I remember it, at this time – have I really reached the age where I start regretting the past and begin to talk drivel? – it snowed every winter and each Christmas a snowman stood guard at the foot of the garden in the blueish light of tumbling snow flakes. The first *cougnolles* arrived a few days before the holidays. On the last day of school, I believe. There must have been something between our mistress and the baker that it was all so co-ordinated. We ate thick slices spread with fresh butter and strawberry jam. They put colour in our cheeks before they were reddened yet more by the wind. Some *cougnolles* were more elaborate representations of little baby Jesus than others. We had ones with a little plaster navel, which fascinated me. Not some kind of a perversion, mind, just greed: I just loved eating the things. Which led me to being perplexed by the anguished but amused cries of my mother oscillating between the fun of telling this to her friends and concern about a resulting gastric perforation. Anyhow, rest easy: plaster is not poisonous, at least not in this quantity. Today, *cougnolles* increasingly come with a whole mini-baby-Jesus, made of sugar or raisins or chocolate, planted on the top of the bun. It's one remove from the classic, but still part of that tradition, and likewise is developing its own cultural following.

© Willy Coppens

Les Mignonettes

OK, so these little chocolate wonders may not be truly Belgian, but the company that makes them, Côte d'Or, certainly used to be – until taken over by the Swiss company Suchard in 1987, only itself to be gobbled up by the US consortium Kraft Foods in 1990. Nevertheless and notwithstanding, a Mignonette and a cup of coffee are as much a part of Belgium culture as watching the TV news at 7:30pm, or eating *pistolet* buns on a Sunday morning (see page 128). Let's not try to hide the fact that, basically, we are all addicted to Mignonettes, and mainly the milk chocolate ones in the red wrapper.

First scenario: shopping with the wife and a brief break in a respectable little café to rest her feet. Two coffees, please. They arrive. Add milk and sugar to the coffee according to taste, and without delay take hold of the little red rectangle. Above all, do not allow it to melt against the hot cup. Open it. I could say 'delicately', but there is no need, because this sweet morsel of confectionary has been devised to unwrap itself with the flick of a nail, without resistance. Take the first sip of coffee, at this stage generally still a tad too hot, and bite into the Mignonette. In just two mouthfuls, alas, it's all over. Finish your coffee and gently float the idea of cutting short the shopping and heading for home.

Second scenario: at home. There is a more elaborate product at our disposition, compromising a range of Mignonettes: dark chocolate, milk chocolate, coffee-flavoured chocolate, chocolate with hazelnuts – all temptingly presented in a long and satisfyingly heavy box. The pleasure is no longer limited: you can eat the whole lot. What joy!

Third scenario: a little bonus at work, whatever your field. There'll be a birthday, and a colleague will turn up with a box of Mignonettes to celebrate.

© belgiumtheplaceto.be TM - J Jeanmart

Truth be told, there are plenty of situations when a box of Mignonettes is the answer, and it's been like that since 1935, the date when the product was launched on the Belgian market. Ah, the comfort of constancy in our changing world!

Le Spéculoos

© belgiumtheplaceto.be TM - J Jeanmart

I challenge you to find a Belgian who has never eaten *spéculoos.*

Yes, a Belgian who is just a few days old, OK; or maybe someone who was abandoned in a forest and raised by a pack of wolves. Outside these two extremes, I cannot see how a Belgian worthy of the name could be entirely unaware of the taste of *spéculoos* and not be addicted to it… OK, OK, I'm talking about myself here, but, hey, I know I am not alone.

Normally, the pattern develops as follows. During its first year of life, a baby will experience at least one Fête de Saint-Nicolas (6 December) – it's unavoidable – during which his granddad or grandma will not be able to stop themselves giving it the latest Fisher-Price toy plus a big image of Saint-Nicolas of Myra (the original Santa Claus) and perhaps also his sidekick Père Fouettard – brought along to whip the naughty children – made of the hard, cinnamon-flavoured biscuit called *spéculoos.*

It's the beginning of the end. The baby will chew on it, marvelling at it and dribbling brown fluid on its bib. Using its gums or its milk teeth, depending how the building site in its mouth is progressing, it will be in seventh heaven and will have no trouble demolishing the entire Saint Nicholas. And so the habit is formed.

Christmas comes again and, step by step, the young will dip their *spéculoos* into their grenadine drink, then their Coca-Cola, then their coffee, or – in the case of supporters of Belgium's national football team, the Red Devils , into their beer. Yes, *spéculoos* accompanies Belgians through every step of their lives.

The kind I have just been talking about are the miniature, pocket-sized *spéculoos,* but there are also big-scale *spéculoos,* the size of a dining table or just about. Made in the form of religious figures, they are shaped in wooden moulds commissioned from specialist wood carvers. A celebrated purveyor of these things, along with other traditional Belgian biscuits – such as the sugar-coated *pain à la grecque* and deliciously crumbly, butter-rich *sablés* biscuits – is the Maison Dandoy in Brussels. Any Belgian might find themselves alternating these high-end delights with supermarket *spéculoos* by Lotus in order to remain firmly in touch with the treasured flavours of Belgian childhood.

Les Chokotoffs

Belgian TV viewers in the 1980s will remember the advert. The comely young woman on her deckchair voluptuously sucks on her Chokotoff, giving herself up to pleasure. The sun sets, and when she comes to, she removes her sunglasses to reveal white patches around her eyes, while the rest her face is deeply bronzed. The message from Côte d'Or, manufacturers of these caramel-filled chocolates, is that a Chokotoff will cast you off into dreamland, where time stands still. But I would suggest the opposite. Because when I eat a Chokotoff my experience is precisely the reverse. Time whips by, and in a flash I have eaten about 10 in a row and the packet is empty – even if I seem to have opened it just a moment ago. However, it is true, I admit, a Chokotoff does have a chewy side. It provokes a goodly flow of saliva which it busily contrives to direct towards the vocal cords, especially when you're in a group, and mucks about with them royally. The taste is inimitable, and matched only by the firmness of its bite. While taking all this into consideration, I still fail to understand quite how I manage to eat them so quickly. I think I must eat several at a time. I just don't know: I'm a bit brain-dead at such moments, but – I tell myself – maybe it's just a question of doing more training.

© belgiumtheplaceto.be TM - J Jeanmart

Sugar pie -
La Tarte au Sucre

There is *tarte au sucre* and *tarte au sucre,* and I don't intend to sow discord between the various communities who claim true ownership. Let me clearly state that the *tarte au sucre* of Charleroi is not better than that of Chaumont-Gistoux, nor indeed that of any other Belgian town or village, and vice versa. Agreed?

Now we've got that straight, let's have a look at these various *tartes au sucre* – sugar tarts, literally made of pure sugar. The Charleroi *tarte au sucre* uses fine white sugar, and not *cassonade* (fine-grained, light brown sugar). Once upon a time, white sugar was the most chic, because it was the most refined – in both senses of the word. This is well before we started to pay a premium for a return to Nature and to revel in the health benefits of organic and whole foods…

The province of Walloon Brabant also has its traditional *tarte au sucre* – brown and made with *cassonade.* Prepared and eaten according to the rules of the art, it is made in Chaumont-Gistoux, Wavre and Waterloo where the august Confrérie des Maîtres Paveûs, Scribeux et Mougneux de la Tarte au Sucre (Brotherhood of the Master Workers, Writers and Eaters of Sugar Tarts) sees it as its mission to spread the word about this wondrous product to anyone who will listen.

So you see, there's *tarte au sucre and tarte au sucre.* The same applies to cane sugar. Not to mention our very own beet sugar. Whatever the origin, I would happily sign up to any brotherhood of *tarte au sucre* enthusiasts, because – gracious me! – this stuff is good!

- To create the filling for a *tarte au sucre de Charleroi,* beat an egg with two tablespoons of white sugar and a little ground cinnamon.

© belgiumtheplaceto.be TM - J Jeanmart

- Spread this over your base of shortcrust pastry, and sprinkle with more white sugar.
- Leave to rise for half and hour before baking, so that the pastry becomes impregnated with the sugar mix.
- Place in a hot oven. The tart is cooked when the sugar becomes caramelised. Remove and sprinkle with a little more white sugar, to create little light-coloured islands melting in the darker caramel. Divine!

Les Croustillons

There's no single word for *croustillant* or *croustillon* in English, but it evokes something crusty, crisp, crunchy – and deep-fried. It's the kind of food associated with the fairs that hold such a special place in the life of our idyllic land of luxury and plenty. These tasty little mini-doughnuts are a speciality of Liège, and the famous Foire de Liège, or October Fair, is really the only place to taste them. And to appreciate them to the full, you need a backdrop of drizzle or a *drache* (a downpour). Note that we're not talking here about one of those bizarre, semi-tropical summer storms; for that you'd need to be tucking into *croustillons* on the Rue de Roture during the other great Liège festival, the "15 Août en Outremeuse"...

Anyhow, *croustillons* are eaten with a sprinkling of icing sugar, while burning the tips of your fingers at the very least, as well as your mouth. You eat them as you walk along, and end up having to brush yourself down. And sucking the end of each finger meticulously before discarding the carton. In a bin, please!

FOR 4 PEOPLE

20g plain flour, 15g fresh yeast, 100ml whole milk, 1 tsp caster sugar, 100ml light beer, 1 egg, 25g butter, 1 pinch of salt, icing sugar, oil for deep-frying (e.g. groundnut or sunflower)

- Warm the milk, add the sugar, and stir the yeast into this mix.
- Sieve the flour into this mix, add the yolk of the egg, the salt, the beer and the melted butter.
- Beat the egg white until fluffy and firm, and fold this into the mix.
- Cover with a cloth and allow to rest of about 30 minutes, until it has doubled in size.

© belgiumtheplaceto.be TM - J Jeanmart

- Heat the oil to 180°C.
- Using two teaspoons, make little balls of dough, then fry them in the oil for one minute.
- Drain on kitchen paper. Serve sprinkled with icing sugar.

Materne Jam

Culture is like jam: the less you have of it, the more thinly you have to spread it. On the culture side, I'm lucky, can't complain. You probably noticed. By contrast, on the jam side, often I have a hard time of it, and if there is one thing that I really detest spreading, it's the bottom of a jar of Materne strawberry jam. Only to achieve a pale rose colour on my buttered slice of bread. It drives me nuts! The bottom of a Materne jar is designed in such a way that it is virtually impossible to extract the last grams on the point of a knife. You have to equip yourself with a spoon. Yes, OK, I know, you should use a spoon to get jam out of a jar in any case, but you have to admit that you yourself don't always do that, do you. And while we're on the subject, why don't you also admit that you sometimes lick your knife? A fault confessed is a fault half redressed. But to come back to the bottoms of jars, you need a spoon, sure, but what then? Spread it on a slice of bread? No, I think not, sir! That borders on the ridiculous. Straight in the mouth. Only good can come of it. I was talking about it with my psychiatrist just this instant.

Materne jam – in its trademark triangular jars – is an institution in Belgium. The company was founded in Wépion, home of Belgian strawberries (see page 46) by Édouard Materne in 1888; since 1980 it's been made in Floreffe, west of Namur. In my home, that's to say my home when I was a child, it was the only jam that was considered worthy of a place next to our homemade jams in the kitchen cupboard. Rhubarb and apricot, and pure rhubarb, were the family specialities. We also had strawberries, but we ate them fresh with sugar, so for jam, that never happened… I loved the rhubarb jam, but I was rather less keen on the cellophane that covered the pots. It was fun to put on when helping out, armed with elastic bands and a little sponge to dampen the paper, but afterwards it took on a life of its own well before the pot was finished. On the Materne pot, by

© belgiumtheplaceto.be TM - J Jeanmart

contrast, there was the screw-lid. Oh, joy! Inside, big lumps of strawberry and liquid jam. On a slice of *craquelin* bread spread with fresh butter, there's nothing better for a child's after-school tea-time snack. That's one thing I really miss from my school days. Another subject for discussion with my psychiatrist.

Brazilian pie –
La Tarte brésilienne

What exactly is a *tarte brésilienne?* Or a simply *'brésilienne'* – as everyone in Belgium knows what you mean when you say *'brésilienne'* without having to specify the *'tarte.'* But although they know it, few can say precisely what it is.

Did it really come with the samba and the tango in the days of our spotty youth from far-away South America, or Brazil to be more precise? Seems unlikely. My doubt may surprise you as you'll know by now that in general I'm pretty credulous, not to say gullible. All we know is that all these *tartes brésiliennes* have been dancing out of our bakeries and tearooms ever since Belgium became Belgium. It would seem that the origin of the name has vanished into the cream and the nuts.

Note that a true *tarte brésilienne* is flan-filled, topped with a layer of fresh cream beaten with sugar, and covered with caramelised nuts (you can buy commercially prepared, caramelised crushed nuts called *brésiliennes* to sprinkle on the top). But you will have encountered, or one day will encounter, false *brésiliennes* which have traded their flan filling for creamed rice or *crème pâtissière*. Keep to your path, do not be seduced: they are for the tourists.

© belgiumtheplaceto.be TM - J Jeanmart

Chocolate Éclairs

What? Chocolate éclairs? Surely they are international, and with a name like that you might guess French? Ah, yes, but in Belgium they are better: *crème pâtissière* on the inside, dark Belgian chocolate outside. We'll come to that. But first, have you ever wondered about the origin of the name of this splendid little piece of pâtisserie? No, well, maybe not: maybe you are happy just to scoff the things, and I can't say I blame you. In fact, I'd never really thought about this, until the children posed the question. Well, first off, *éclair* in French means lightning, as of thunder, and flash of. Lightning and speed. Yes indeed. It is thought that the inspiration for the name of this wondrously light and fluffy pâtisserie was indeed the speed at which is can be consumed.

First comes the choux pastry, superlight and tasty… hmmm, a delight in itself. Next there's the *crème pâtissière,* which, when suitably rich and creamy, is the kind of thing that might persuade you to sell your soul to the devil. Finally the chocolate icing. When it is fine and soft and does not stick to the roof of your mouth, it is sheer pleasure. For me, chocolate éclairs are a weakness. Everything in moderation, they say, but oh! with chocolate éclairs my resistance collapses, and I fall to the sin of gluttony with the speed that is their name.

© belgiumtheplaceto.be TM - J Jeanmart

Le Massepain

Massepain should not be confused with marzipan (which is *pâte d'amandes* in French). It might seem that they are basically the same thing, give or take a few almonds. But no, not if you know *massepain*. The difference is that, properly made, *massepain* is a luxury product, a delicious confectionery to be savoured on its own. You would not dream of plastering it on a cake.

They share a similar derivation, of course. The history of the word is surprisingly complex. One theory is that it is derived from the Arabic word *mawthaban*, meaning 'someone who sits still in a majestic manner'. This was also the word for a Byzantine coin which was used at the time of the Crusades in the Levant region of the Middle East; one side showed Christ enthroned, hence the name. In about 1193, the Venetians started to use a similar coin called a 'matapanus', which they stored in small boxes made for the purpose. The coins went out of circulation, but the boxes – still named after the coins – remained. In the 14th century, this became the name for what was put inside such a box: a confectionery made of sugar, almonds and rosewater. After this, *massepain* spread across Western Europe.

In southwest France, in Périgord, a *massepain* is a form of pâtisserie resembling a savoy cake, but in nearby Quercy it's quite another thing. In the Netherlands, it's the preferred medium for making Saint Nicholas figurines for Christmas. And in Belgium? Well, in Belgium it is presented in its pure form of sweetened ground almonds, often as a log of 250g and 500g. It is a winter treat, associated with Christmastide and New Year's Eve festivities, and goes with the clementines, *spéculoos* biscuits, a carrot and a beer that you put out each evening for Saint Nicholas and his black pal Père Fouettard (a.k.a. Zwarte Piet) around 6 December. It gets eaten bit by bit in thin slices, in cubes or in little balls – constantly nibbled away, almost imperceptibly. It is one of the most promising fuels for perpetual motion: people come and go continually.

© Boulangerie Vienne

There are variants of *massepain* where pistachios are added, or walnuts, or anything dry. Sometimes too, it is presented in the form of some ridiculous creature, such as a pink pig. But the only true and truly unique *massepain* is beige, and made of almonds and sugar alone. There are different ways to eat it too: grilled, or – but this is really perverse – hot, having been baked in the oven. It's the kind of thing that takes about five years to digest.

La Frangipane

This a word that confuses English speakers. It sounds like the exotic tree, the frangipani, with its sweet-perfumed flowers. But no. That was named after the 16th-century Italian Marquis of Frangipani. This frangipane is something quite different, a rich cake mixture based on ground almonds. And what would the Belgians be without their frangipane? A mere shadow of themselves, I imagine. For these inveterate gourmands eat frangipane year in, year out, as every *pâtissier* fully understands. The Belgians and almonds: it's a love story.

To make frangipane you do indeed need almonds. Ground almonds, needless to say: whole almonds would be a bit lumpy. Ground almonds, sugar, eggs and butter. A drop or two of good dark rum never goes amiss, but not Barcardi, of course, which would put a dent in the whole enterprise.

You are also going to need some *pâte feuilletée* – usually translated as puff pasty, but the *pâte feuilletée* of the Belgian *pâtissier's* art is so much more delightfully flaky. Plus a tart or cake tin, and an oven, and voilà, you are ready for a great adventure. But the easiest way to do this is just to go to a good *pâtissier*, to avoid the risk of disappointment.

The most famous of all Belgian frangipane cakes contain a *fève* (bean) – like a dried haricot bean. Best not to swallow it, though: first because the traditional bean has usually been replaced by a small porcelain or plastic figurine; and second because the person who finds the bean in their slice gets to wear the crown which comes with the cake. For this is the *galette des Rois* (Kings' cake), eaten to mark Epiphany on 6 January, when the Magi visited the baby Jesus. It's a Belgian institution, a celebration to mark the closing days of Christmas – when there's always good reason to crown a new king or a queen.

La mousse au chocolat

French, yes – but also so typically *belge* too, and so well made in our royal kingdom! There are not a lot of us in my family, and back home it's the men who do the cooking. Well, not me: I've chosen other pursuits. I write, for example. Anyhow, all this to explain that what I am about to give you is my brother's secret recipe. When it was my father making it, I would manage to stick a finger in without anyone noticing, but it made by fingernails dirty – a bit of a giveaway. I'm wiser now: I only take a sneak preview when my brother makes white chocolate mousse. Shhhh! Don't tell a soul!

So, *mousse au chocolat* for 10 people. Well, why not? Why do recipes only cater for 4? How do they manage in large families? Here small families will just have to do the sums, and anyway no one complains of having too much *mousse au chocolat!*

- 10 egg yolks, 10 whites of egg, 250g sugar, 1 litre fresh cream, 500g dark chocolate with 70% cocoa content.

THE BEST WAY TO PREPARE IT

- Mix the yolks with half the sugar until thick and pale, and the mixture falls back on itself like a slowly dissolving ribbon.
- Melt the chocolate in a pan, on its own, in a bain-marie.
- Whisk the egg whites until they form soft peaks, then sprinkle on the remainder of the sugar and beat the mixture to form stiff peaks.
- Whip the cream into soft peaks (when the whisk starts to leave furrows, it's just about there).
- Stir the chocolate into the egg yolk mixture.
- Fold this mixture into the whisked egg white.

© belgiumtheplaceto.be TM - J Jeanmart

- Now fold in the whipped cream.
- Allow to rest for an hour.

THE BEST WAY TO EAT IT

- Take a decent-sized finger, preferably a middle one.
- Check that it does not bear any family heirlooms or other jewellery.
- Dip the finger into the mousse up to the second joint (more would be excessive).
- Don't forget to bend the finger before taking it out of the pot, so as to extract the maximum load.
- Lift this to your mouth, suck the finger well, before repeating the process.
- For sensitive souls, I recommend a *langue de chat* (cat tongue) biscuit or, at a pinch, for those on a diet, a coffee spoon.
- But you have to admit that it really does not taste as good like that.

Le Huit

Huit: the name means 'eight'. It does not take a genius to work out why: the photo contains a clue. Come to think of it, it probably didn't take a genius to name it in the first place. Anyhow, I have always had a personal affinity for the number eight. Firstly, because it was on the eighth day of a month that I cried out to the world for the first time, and have never stopped since (I suggest that we should celebrate the 8th of every month, instead of settling for just once a year). Secondly, because infinity is an 8 having a lie-down; to eat a *huit* you have to turn it in the direction of infinity, which makes me think that when another birthday comes round, there will be another after that – which is very reassuring for gourmands. Lastly, because it concerns a totally surreal kind of pastry.

Allow me to explain. Consider: when you first clamp eyes on this thing, you can see it's not going to be easy to eat. You are going to need to lick your fingers countless times, even to wash your hands, once done. A *huit* is more a baker's thing than a *pâtissier's*. It's associated more with croissants and *pistolet* rolls (see page 128) than with frangipane (page 98) and *merveilleux* (page 101), positioning it with breakfast rather than dessert. Which means that a *huit* is more likely to be carried in a bag than in a box, and is eaten without the aid of cutlery. They are messy, unwieldy, awkward, the ugly ducklings of the bakery world: that's what's surreal about them. My heart goes out to them when I see them piled up high in the bakery sections of our supermarkets: as a result, fearing the suffering that will be inflicted by the separation of these Siamese twins, I simply cannot stop myself buying them.

Now let's take a closer look at a *huit*. The basic structure is puff pasty, filled with *crème pâtissière* coated with fruit syrup, and a sugar glaze on the pastry. Pretty ordinary, you might say. But have you ever

© La pâtisserie Eggenols

turned a *huit* over? What can you see? The *crème pâtissière* holds its position without support. That's pretty weird, no? Completely surreal. It fills the empty space, but never falls out. While it is quite possible that, when you bite into it, a few pieces will fall out, if you take a complete *huit* and shake it, the *crème* will remain curled in the centre of the two circles. This leaves me speechless at the wonder of it: how can it be possible?

This is an appeal to all *huit*-eaters in Belgium: turn them over, if only once in your life, and admire this phenomenon. After that, you may swallow them whole if you wish, but I will be happy for I will know – even if you protest – that I have taught you something.

Le Merveilleux

Only in Belgium could you invent a pâtisserie with a name like this: *merveilleux* means 'marvellous'. Two discs of meringue, a little Chantilly cream between them, and chocolate shavings all over the outside. What could be more simple? Some chichi types will a put a maraschino cherry on the top, a tedious gesture that adds nothing to the splendidly simple flavours of the original concept. I also know of dangerous maniacs who replace the chocolate shavings with a whole curled leaf of chocolate, for *le look,* as they say. Idiots! It masks the soft folds of cream and its virginal whiteness, and unbalances the effect with too much chocolate. I won't even begin to describe to you those certifiable idiots on conditional release who make frozen *merveilleux,* with kiwi or blackcurrant sorbet or some other unnamed horror in place of the cream.

The most divine *merveilleux* – isn't it magnificent to be able to describe a food as a 'divine *merveilleux*'? That has to be one of the greatest of all those linguistic oddities that we like to call 'belgicisms'! – should be eaten by a distinguished old lady in what passes for a hat, sitting in a slightly down-at-heel tearoom lit by neon, drinking teabag tea. She nibbles at her treat, her lower lip extended in expectation, and from time to time she tosses a crumb as an offering to her little poodle-god hovering at her feet. And then, with trembling finger, she attacks the flared paper stamped with the *pâtissier's* name to lick up the last happy moments of the day before tottering back to her home and an evening with the television.

Le Cha-Cha

Before all else, hang on just a moment! A bit of history: I'm trying to find out when this little treat first saw the light of day. But *zut!*, it's not written on the wrapper. OK, I'll have a look at another, perhaps I'll have more luck here. *Zut* again! That's terrible! Still no info. I am vaguely reminded of that German kid in *Charlie and the Chocolate Factory*, Augustus Gloop. You know, the one who guzzles bar after bar of chocolate in the quest to find a Golden Ticket. I'm saying that for the benefit of those who know their classics. And talking of classics, the Cha-Cha is a fine example of one. There's no point looking for its date of birth: the Cha-Cha is timeless, eternal, older than you, older than me, older than our dads, older than time itself. No point, either, trying to find it beyond our borders.

The Cha-Cha is Belgian. How could it not be? OK so they are now made by LU, a French company owned by Kraft, but as they themselves say: the Cha-Cha is *'pour les vrais belges'* (for true Belgians) and 'a perfect combination of crispy mini-waffle *(gaufrette croustillante)* filled with caramel and coated in good chocolate.' Talk about ticking all the Belgian boxes! The only way to be sure of eating any beyond our borders is to fill your pockets and suitcases with them, and to resist that burning desire to eat the lot one after the other before you leave, Augustus Gloop-style.

Les beignets aux pommes

Doughnuts, waffles, fritters, *croustillons, lacquemants* – ah, how the Belgians love all sweet things made of batter, and sprinkled with fine sugar!

These are all quintessential holiday and fairground treats. However, *beignets aux pommes* – apple fritters – are more typically family fare. For winter days of short afternoons when night falls at teatime at the end of the school day. That's the time to peel the apples. At the house of one of my grandmothers we had to go up into the loft, using a torch. The electrical wiring did not stretch that far. There were cobwebs and a sickly-sweet smell in the air. That of the apples. Hundreds of apples stored for the winter. We had been eating them all summer, even so, and tens of kilos had been sent to the apple press. We had enough juice to withstand a siege. The winter apples were different. Much less juicy, but still full of flavour. These were the ones used for *beignets* and tarts.

For the *beignets*, I could make the batter. Only the batter, though: frying is far too dangerous when you are 'as tall as three apples', as the expression goes.

THE RECIPE WAS SO SIMPLE

250g plain flour, ½ cube (10g) of baker's yeast, 1 tbsp oil, 1 egg, warm water, 4 apples, oil for deep-frying (e.g. groundnut or sunflower), sugar

- Sieve the flour into a bowl.
- Make a well in it and put in the oil and the yeast dissolved in a little warm water.
- Mix with a spatula while adding enough warm water to obtain a batter just thick enough to fall back on itself like a slowly dissolving ribbon.
- Beat the white of the egg for a minute, then add it to the mix.
- Leave to rest for 2 hours.
- Peel and core the apples, and cut them into evenly shaped rings.
- Put them in the batter.
- Heat the oil.
- Lift an apple ring with batter attached and drop it into the oil.
- Allow it to take colour until golden brown.
- Drain, sprinkle with sugar and serve.

Sometimes, to inject an additional festive note, the apple pieces were first left to soak in dark rum. Why not, I say!

Les gosettes

What's difficult about a *gosette* is not buying it or eating it, but eating it when driving. Why am I talking about that? Do I hear you object? Clearly you haven't bought one or several still-warm *gosettes* and placed them next to you on the passenger seat. Am I right? Hence your objection. Try it, you'll see.

First of all there is the smell gently filtering through the paper bag. Then there's your stomach, which makes its degree of deprivation known through the volume of its rumbling. Finally there is some kind of traffic jam at the edge of town which starts to get on your nerves. This is fatal, if you have a normal constitution: your eyes will be drawn more and more to the passenger seat. It's either or. Either you have bought only one *gosette,* for your own consumption. It will therefore be easy to cede to the temptation there and then. Or you have several specimens at your disposal, bought for an afternoon snack among colleagues, friends, children or even a lover. If the quantity can tolerate the loss of one, you won't hesitate. If the contrary is the case, this is a terrible dilemma. You could eat one, but you would have to turn around in heavy traffic and head back to the bakery to make up the numbers, or you could exert masterly self-control, but you could perforate a stomach ulcer with the stress.

So, to come back to my initial proposition: what is difficult is eating a *gosette* while driving. I didn't foresee this long digression about the passenger seat, but you insidiously led me into it. Thanks for that. And I haven't even explained what a *gosette* is: in brief, it's a kind of turnover made with puff-pastry filled with apples, cherries or apricots. Eating a *gosette* while driving is a fool's game: if it is a tiny bit warm, so the apples, cherries or apricots melt in the mouth, at one moment or another a catastrophe will occur and your immaculate shirt will be punished. It's inevitable. Then everything starts to go haywire, and you kick yourself and swear that next time you'll put the things in the boot because, damn it, they're just too darn good!

© belgiumtheplaceto.be TM - J Jeanmart

La Boule de Berlin

Bouuuuuuuuuuuuuuuuuuuuuuuuullllllllllllllle… de Beeeeeeerliiiiiiiiiiiiiiiiiiiiiiin! I have never understood why the salesman, carrying his tray along the shore, uses this term. *Boule de Berlin.* All I know is that this marvel of pâtisserie carries the same sweet name even in Portugal. It bugs me. Sometimes as I lie awake at night, I wonder what these delicious things are called in Berlin. Well yes, we never ask that kind of question, and indeed, there's some good questions to be answered here. Like, what is a Salade Niçoise called in Nice? A hamburger in Hamburg?

Well, anyhow, let's get back to the *boule.* It's a doughnut-like thing, relatively substantial, filled with an artificial *crème pâtissière,* and it's the delight of hol daymakers both big and small in the Kingdom of Belgium. To really appreciate *boules de Berlin* you must have hands smeared with sun cream. Don't laugh: even in Belgium you have to use sun cream. With climate change, the data will change, as will the location of the coast no doubt, but we'll still be talking about *boules de Berlin* in Volume 29 of *A Slice of Belgium,* I guarantee. So, if your fingers are not covered in sun cream, hurry along and find some, or your *boule de Berlin* will just not taste the same. And to be truly authentic, you must absolutely toss in a few grains of sand, which stick to the sun cream, and give a *boule* a bit of crunch.

Once all the preliminary conditions have been met, you will finally be in possession of your *boule de Berlin.* Careful now: this is the moment of truth. Don't forget that it's best first to remove all the hair from the lower part of your body, regardless of your gender, before you start eating. Because there is nothing more painful than pulling out your hairs to remove the *crème pâtissière* that inevitably escapes from the *boule.*

© belgiumtheplaceto.be TM - J Jeanmart

When at last you have finally finished it, don't forget to suck your fingers voluptuously. That's the moment when the taste of sun cream really comes to the fore. But if your name is Lolita, don't do this while eyeing up the old man sitting close by: that's just mean.

Laurent Gerbaud:
Chocolatier

'I swear to God,' declares Laurent Gerbaud's website, 'our chocolates do contain no added sugar, no butter, no gin [he means alcohol], no preservative, no artificial flavour, no additive'. My goodness, can it contain anything at all? Well yes, chocolate pure and simple – and it is this purist approach that has sent Laurent Gerbaud rocketing into the high firmament of Belgian *chocolatiers* since he opened his first shop in Brussels in 2009. And that is some dizzying firmament, I don't need to tell you! And all in the complete absence of *pralines* – the filled chocolates for which Belgium is (justly) famed! Instead, Laurent Gerbaud's plain and milk chocolate is made into slabs or truffles, or used to coat fruits and nuts.

A degree in medieval history and a prolonged stay in China led Laurent Gerbaud to his distinctive approach to chocolate-making. In his efforts to set up a chocolate business in Shanghai, he began to explore less sweet flavours to suit the local market, and to experiment with exotic citrus fruits such the kumquats, yuzu and bergamot. Inventive flavours are his hallmark, all carefully researched and judged. Dark chocolate bars spiced with pepper corns, Persian cranberries, and sweet chilli; bars of crystallized ginger riding on little chocolate strips; chocolate-coated plums, pears, figs, coffee beans, *spéculoos* biscuits; orangettes (slivers of candied orange coated in chocolate), citronnettes (lemon), pamplemouse (grapefruit). It's an Aladdin's cave of taste!

Everything is carefully sourced, especially the raw chocolate itself, prepared by the specialist Italian company Domori of Turin, and mixed for the 75% dark chocolate, for instance, from Trinitario beans from Madagascar and Forastero beans from Ecuador. Rigorously controlled low temperatures – permissible only with low-volume production – preserve the delicate flavours.

© Laurent Gerbaud

These days you can buy Laurent Gerbaud chocolates in numerous specialist outlets in Brussels and abroad. But if you want to get to the heart of the matter, go to his headquarters shop in the Rue Ravenstein in Brussels, where you may even get to see the chocolate-making process in action – or try it for yourself by joining a workshop.

That list of no-nos, citing what Laurent Gerbaud's chocolates do not contain, ends with *'mais plein d'amour* – but full of love'. See them, smell them, taste them: you can believe it!

© belgiumtheplaceto.be TM - J Jeanmart

10. Granny's comfort food

La Chicorée

'Who has drunk…will drink… Chicorée Pacha,' goes the slogan. If you haven't come across it, that's because you are too young, or too new to Belgium. The large, cylindrical, orange packets, with the drawing of the Ottoman Pasha on the front – that's a slice of our domestic history, even if, since 1992 it's been French (acquired by Chicorée Leroux). Chicory is and remains the poor man's coffee, Northerners' coffee, wartime coffee. It's also the perfect complement to *'café chaussette'* (filter bag coffee) and even percolated coffee: it gives the coffee a more caramelised, fruity flavour. Soluble or instant chicory, simply mixed into milk with sugar, brought comfort throughout my entire childhood. My cousins and I used to drink this at my grandmother's cottage. With its flavour of hazelnuts and its sweetness, it was magnificent. Well, perhaps it was not quite as wonderful as that, but this was the taste of my childhood, and for that reason alone it is magnificent. In a milkshake too, it's a complete joy. I think I have detected this flavour in some American coffees, in some of the things Starbucks does, with milk or cold. Clearly I'm in a state of full-on regression – and I'm not sure what to make of it!

© belgiumtheplaceto.be TM - J Jeanmart

La frisée aux lardons

The life of a gastronome is a magnificent and harmonious mixture of things, some easy, some hard. Take a dish like *L'oie à l'instar de Visé* (goose cooked to a recipe of Visé, a town on the River Meuse, in the Province of Liège): everyone agrees that this is a real test for any chef, and hence by extension of any overstressed mother with a family to feed. At the other end of the scale, take *Pêche au thon* (see page 75): few people are incapable of creating this chef-d'oeuvre of Belgian gastronomy. The only real difficulty could arise from the lack of a stool or kitchen steps to permit a small person (you can make this dish from the age of five upwards) to get at tins stored on the upper shelves of the cupboard. *Frisée aux lardons* clearly belongs in this second category, and no cookbook would ever place it higher than 'suitable for idiots'. And yet it's not as simple as that, and, for a successful outcome, a number of factors have to be brought into play – and chance isn't one of them.

For a start, forget that frisée lettuce that been wilting in the vegetable compartment of your fridge since your big weekly shop last Saturday: put on your rollerblades and slip down to the nearest quality greengrocer to buy a fresh one. While you are at it, glide along to the butcher and get some slices of decent bacon: surely you're not contemplating shoving a pile of those pre-packaged pink and white lumps they call lardons in your salad bowl?

So here you are, in your socks, the rollerblades lying about in the entrance of the room constituting an evil trap and future subject of dispute when your beloved other half returns, your eyes now fixed on the beautiful frisée lettuce sitting on the worktop. Armed with a knife, go for the heart. That's the bit to keep. Reject the dark outer leaves; chuck them in the bin, alongside last Saturday's frisée. While your chopped lardons sizzle in the pan, cut up and strip down the

© belgiumtheplaceto.be TM - J Jeanmart

tender heart of the lettuce. Lardons, chopped shallots, bits of cooked potato, walnut halves or croutons – whatever you fancy – can be happily tossed in amongst the greenery, in a big salad bowl. For the seasoning, mustard and vinegar are essential. For the exquisite final touch, deglaze the pan with a little raspberry vinegar, and tip this over the mix. Hmmm… that's making me salivate just to think about it. But my fridge has none of the ingredients to satisfy my desire. Quick, get those rollerblades on! Let the great adventure begin (never mind that it's raining).

Le Boudin-compote-purée (and other boudins)

So, what is the secret of this dish that wins the hearts of generation after generation of Belgian children. That's right – children! The *boudin* here is *boudin noir,* a soft kind of blood sausage or 'black pudding'. The *compote* is an apple purée, and (just to complicate things) the *purée* is mashed potato. And Belgian children love it! Me, I would start salivating the moment I got a whiff of the sizzling *boudin* rising through my home, and now it's my children whose mouths start watering as I stand over the stove, armed with my potato masher and a slab of butter.

Boudin noir – one of the most ancient of all sausages – has a noble history among the farms and rural areas of our land. Originally it was made just before Christmas, when pigs were traditionally slaughtered as they reached their fattest, just as the weather turned really cold. These days there's no longer a fixed time for killing pigs – well, of course you don't want to set about it in the middle of the night: you'll wake the neighbours. No, what I mean is there's no longer a fixed season for *boudin,* because now you can buy it at any butcher's, or indeed supermarket, throughout the year. But originally this was well and truly associated with Christmas – a hearty dish to tuck into after a cold walk home from Midnight Mass. And even now sales of *boudin* still rocket around Christmas time.

Boudin noir is made from fresh blood, which is immediately salted on slaughter to prevent coagulation and then stuffed into casings or 'skins' (*tripes* in French), made of cleaned and boiled intestines.

Boudin blanc, on the other hand, looks like a soft white version of the same thing but is in fact a rather different beast altogether. Here the filling consists of a mixture of bread and lean pork, plus milk and egg, and the sausage is boiled in water to complete its preparation. This was eaten by country folk – cold, grilled or fried – throughout the year and was not particularly linked to Christmas festivities, although some *boudin de Noël* is white.

Onion and spices are standard ingredients in both sorts, *noir* and *blanc,* but there are many other kinds of elaborations on these themes, involving apples, leeks, chestnuts, mushrooms, raisins, apricots, truffles, kirsch, calvados, *spéculoos,* you name it. No holds barred! Butchers who specialise in *boudins* all have their special recipes, jealously guarded – and some make *boudins* in 30 different varieties. In Wallonia the traditional name is *tripes:* look out, for instance, for *tripes à l'djote,* made with Swiss chard.

Nowadays, *boudin-compote-purée* is a feast to be enjoyed whenever you please. To really make an occasion of it, get the children to help you cut up the apples, then – rather than making a slightly sweetened purée (also good!) – fry them gently in a knob of fresh better. Belgian kids will have had practice at that at their nursery schools, and are only too happy to demonstrate their cordon bleu skills back at home. Same goes for the mashed potato. Work it with love, without skimping on the butter, while the *boudin noir* sizzles gently in the pan. Then *hop! à table!* Warning: with a dish as mouth-watering as this, there's always a high risk of burnt mouths. But if you're really in a hurry, feel free to blow on your loaded fork!

Le Steak-frites-salade

No need to get into a long culinary dissertation on the attraction that all normally configured Belgians feel for a nice bit of beef. For these good people, who are quite likely to swoon over classic meaty Belgian fare such as *carbonnades flamandes* (beef stewed in beer) and *filet américain* (see page 72), will never turn up their noses at a good steak cooked to their specification and accompanied by a tasty salad and heap of golden chips *(frites)*. Is there any restaurant in Belgium that does not have this on its menu? OK, I see you countering this with exceptions – Thai restaurants, vegetarian – but let it be said once and for all, tofu is not the preferred foodstuff of the Belgians, but steak is. Heads up, hold on tight: I'm going to shock you now. The important thing about the meat is how it is on the plate! Unfortunately – and I feel that some of you will look at me askance here – the great Belgian Blue cattle do not make the best beef in the world. In my view it is a bit too lean and lacks that pure delectability of Irish beef. What heresy!

You don't really need a recipe to make a steak, just a couple things you have to be aware of. Primo: never, ever put salt on it before the butter has melted into it, or else the meat will lose moisture and become tough. Secundo: wait until the butter has stopped sizzling (you are frying this in butter, aren't you?) before placing the steak in the pan, or else the meat will not be fully sealed, and you risk boiling it in its juices. Season the second side while the steak is cooking. Tertio: don't use the cooking juices as a sauce; burnt butter is really bad for your health, as well as your tastebuds! So discard the butter that has been used for the cooking and melt a knob of fresh butter at the last minute, just before despatch (to seventh heaven). As for the salad, to be a truly Belgian one, it has to be a good old-fashioned, garden lettuce, or, at the limit, an endive lettuce or escarole. Wash it in lots of water, several times, and – if needs be – add salt to the water to get rid of the slugs.

© belgiumtheplaceto.be TM - J Jeanmart

Better without slugs. Dry the salad using a tea towel held by its four corners and shaken vigorously. White wine vinegar, one spoon to four of groundnut oil, a little of salt, and little pepper – and that's all you need for a dressing. Stuff made with balsamic vinegar and olive oil – that's not our game. As for the chips, please refer to page 80, but bear in mind one final note: a salad slightly warmed and ever so slightly wilted by the warmth of the chips – that's surprisingly good.

La cassonade

Cassonade is a kind of golden, granulated sugar invented by the Graeffe family. The word *cassonade* comes from the old, 16th-century term *casson,* which described raw or granulated sugar. In 1929, this Belgian family enterprise became a public company. In 1953 it was acquired by the Raffinerie Tirlemontoise, from Belgium's 'sugar town' of Tienen (Tirlemont in French). Conscious of the sentimental attachment of the consumer to *cassonade,* the new owner decided to keep the name.

The Cassonade Graeffe produced at the sugar refineries of Tienen is obtained by crystallising a mixture of various syrups. Other refineries have now borrowed this name, and you'll see *cassonades* that no longer have any connection with the Belgian original: sometimes it's cane sugar that has been refined just once, or even a white sugar to which molasses – and sometimes flavourings and artificial colours – have been added.

Shhh! One minute – I'm doing some research. But I can't find it. As ever, of course, there's a French name for something that resembles *cassonade.* I can't remember it; I know it's a ridiculous name, which is probably why I have forgotten it. Anyhow, it is of no importance if the French don't know what proper *cassonade* is; what matters is that we Belgians like it. And it's classified as *blonde* or *brune* (light or dark) – just like our beer.

Blonde for *pain perdu* (eggy bread, see page 117), *brune* for crêpes, that's the received wisdom – but personally I really prefer *blonde* on crêpes because it is more silky, while the *brune* melts noticeably better on *pain perdu.* Do as you think best.

Final bit of consumer advice: *la cassonade blonde* on a slice of bread and (salted) butter. The recipe is simple: take a nice slice of white bread, spread it generously with butter, about 3mm thick, then crown this with a layer of *cassonade blonde* about 25mm thick – that's right, about an inch thick! And that's a minimum; with a little experience you could get it up to 35mm. You could also put a bit of *fromage blanc* between the butter and the sugar. If you then wait a few minutes, the moisture in the cheese will spread through the sugar and turn part of it into syrup. Superb!

© belgiumthepaceto.be TM - J Jeanmart

La Piedboeuf brune

This is the beer of childhood for any Walloon over the age of 30. It's the drink of initiation, giving you a taste for the frothy head. It's a sweet, dark beer, with a low-alcohol content (1.2% or 1.5%); today it is made alongside Jupiler at Jupille-sur-Meuse, Liège. The large brown, 75cl bottle has a screw top. It comes out dark as chocolate, with an amber-shaded head.

This was the beer of the boarding school dining hall, where we played at being grown-ups having their first experience of drunkenness. Later we would become nostalgic for the smell of that dining hall, a subtle mix of cheap, stale coffee, cleaning fluids and the remains of yesterday's meals. Of course, in an age where we have started putting bicycle helmets on kids, such a thing with alcohol in it has been removed from schools, and likewise the school dining room itself has often been abolished. For children, fizzy drinks are better, it's been proven. But they can't take memories away.

And then think of all the new mothers, on their first day in the maternity wards of Wallonia and elsewhere, who are given a little of this nectar of the gods to help them produce milk. Everyone agrees that this really makes no difference, but we've got the idea that it's the done thing. A little taste from the very start of childhood, then, since it is already in our mother's milk on that very first day. No better way to inspire brand loyalty has yet been found than a mother's breast.

© belgiumtheplaceto.be TM - J Jeanmart

Brussels sprouts –
les choux de Bruxelles

At the time that you'll be reading these words – and me too in the book that the publisher will have kindly sent to me – the amazing fact that I am about to tell you will have already lost a bit of its appeal. Anyway, I'll press on. It's this: Brussels sprouts – I'm writing about them 'live', here and now. While preparing and cooking them. Picture that! And you are reading the soundtrack.

The secret of cooking Brussels sprouts is to blanch them twice. Blanching removes some of the natural bitterness in this vegetable, and preserves the colour. To blanch them, you need a large quantity of boiling salted water. Immerse the cleaned sprouts just until the water comes back to the boil, remove them and refresh them in cold water. The second time, blanching makes the sprouts more digestible, removing more of that bitterness. Once this has been achieved, you simply cut them in two and fry them in butter.

Speaking of cutting, let me tell you the story of the *Kuulkappers* – the 'cabbage cutters'. Because behind these delicious mini-cabbages lies a fascinating tale. In around 1550 a population explosion in Brussels forced its citizens to expand its market gardening. Despite all their efforts, the growers failed to produce enough vegetables for Brussels. So, in around 1650 our proud ancestors – and in particular those in the community of Saint-Gilles, which lay just outside the city walls – created another variety of cabbage that made it possible to maximize yields from the limited cultivatable land that was available.

On a thick and tough central stem grew 20 to 75 tight little cabbages, attached at the base of their leaves. So Brussels sprouts were born. Now it's just a question of cutting them, just as the Saint-Gillois did with such aplomb, earning themselves the nickname that has stuck to this day: Kuulkappers.

Are we done? OK! Cut!

© belgiumtheplaceto.be TM - J Jeanmart

La Blanquette de veau

Blanquette de veau has nothing to do with the French sparkling wine called Blanquette de Limoux, and indeed the two don't even go well together; nor indeed with Cate Blanchett, although I do sometimes wonder if she has ever eaten her namesake. But she should. If I say that, it's to permit myself a little humour in this otherwise somewhat academic book. After all, laughter is to mankind what *Blanquette de veau* is to the Belgians. Something without which life would barely be worth living.

In brief, in case you are not aware, *Blanquette de veau* is a warming, creamy veal stew – and for a good *blanquette*, you need good veal. Either get good veal, or a good quantity of toothpicks. And for a good *blanquette* it not enough simply to have good veal: you also need the magic touch.

GOOD VEAL, GOOD BLANQUETTE

The secret of a successful *blanquette*, as in many recipes, lies in giving due respect to each of the stages of preparation.

- Start by blanching the meat in water.
- When the water boils, equip yourself with patience and a slotted spoon to skim off all the scum which floats to the surface. Discard the scum.
- Now add the other ingredients: onion, carrot, cloves.
- The vegetables are not going to be discarded, so a bit of scraping and cutting is required.
- The same goes for the meat, since I have to tell you everything.
- Simmer for an hour and a half.
- When the veal is cooked it will break up under the pressure of a fork.
- The sauce is a roux (flour mixed with melted butter) blended with (skimmed) stock from the stew.
- Add to this two egg yokes that have been beaten with cream. Mix.
- Add fried mushrooms.
- I'm cutting this short as it's getting long.
- That's it! Now we're done!
- My mother added little meatballs and chopped gherkins, which made it even nicer.
- But do as you wish. I am merely a spiritual guide on gastronomy's long road, where it is incumbent on everyone to take their second steps alone. I'll hold your hand only for the first.

Le matoufè

Or *matoufet*, as the French spell it; but we'll forget that since this is a traditional Walloon dish. *Matoufè* is a preparation that keeps the body warmer than a neoprene wetsuit or a Gore-Tex one-piece ski outfit. It's the sort of thing you eat before going out to cut a few trees down, or to build a dam to divert a flooded river that is threatening your house, but not if you are planning to doze in front of the TV news, because if you don't immediately burn off the prodigious calories packed into the *matoufè* they'll start burning you.

This peasant fare has been popular in the provinces of Luxembourg, Liège and Namur since the 16th century where it graced the Tupperware lunch boxes of farm labourers as they headed off to work in the fields.

True *matoufè*, the truest of the true, is made with eggs, bacon, milk, flour and biscuits. Onto the fried bacon you pour a mixture of beaten egg, salt, pepper, nutmeg and milk into which a little flour has been stirred. Cook over a high heat, stirring continuously with a fork to break up the pancake-like mass that forms. A pinch of sugar can be added at the same time as a few crushed biscuits stirred into warmed milk. In the Liège region, they don't hold back on the sugar. The creamy *matoufè* is served on a thick slice of bread, or it's taken to the office cold, in a sandwich.

OK, son: thrown back your shoulders, loosen your belt and show us what you're made of!

© belgiumtheplaceto.be TM - J Jeanmart

Le pain perdu

Pain perdu: 'lost bread'. It sounds like bread dropped by Hansel and Gretel in place of white pebbles to leave a trail in the woods, only to be eaten by birds. But no, *pain perdu* is French toast, a.k.a. – in its cruder form – 'eggy bread'. The recipe dates back to times past, when the notion of wastage was unknown. Wise days when using leftovers could be a prelude to a moment of joy.

Pain perdu is first and foremost a smell. The smell of autumn evenings. It appears that we do also eat it on summer evenings, but in my memory it is the smell of autumn that takes precedence. And that of the brown sugar, the *cassonade* (see page 112). As a child I was allowed to soak the slices of stale bread in the milk, and then put them in the egg yoke. When it came to cooking the slices, my mother was in command. I was too small to see what was going on inside the frying pan, but that mysterious higher world bathed me in delicious scents. *Pain perdu,* I've eaten it with my mother, my grandmother and even my great-grandmother. Now I eat it with my children. I suspect them sometimes of putting slices of bread on the radiator to make it go stale. Above all the youngest, who loves munching on those large dark lumps of melted sugar.

© belgiumtheplaceto.be TM - J Jeanmart

Les macaronis au jambon – fromage

If pasta was brought to Europe from China by Marco Polo – who has also subsequently lent his name to the cotton T-shirts that he liked to wear when he gave himself up to the joys of tennis and other outdoor sports – I wonder who had the happy idea of adding ham and cheese (*jambon* and *fromage*). Not to the T-shirts, but to the pasta – just to make that clear. Pasta, in all its forms, is the symbol of Italy. Sure. But some recipes have escaped the attention of our Transalpine cousins. Some of these really annoy them, and the one I'm going to talk to you about is one of those. If you have Italian friends, avoid inviting them to eat *Macaronis au jambon-fromage:* it's a bit like talking to them about the politics of their country, or the economy for that matter; essentially it is one of those subjects that does not contribute to peace and unity among peoples.

Quite where this recipe comes from, there is no way of telling, sad to say, but it doesn't matter as long as you've got the pasta. This *Macaronis* (or *Spaghettis*) *au jambon-fromage* is a classic. No snackbar, no bistrot, no mother of a family (apart from Italian ones, that is), no scout-master, no soldier on manoeuvres fails to make themselves a good plateful of this from time to time. In my home, our recipe is a 'light' version: no cream or milk. Let me explain. Rather that beefing up the dish with a light béchamel sauce, my grandmother quickly made a *beurre manié* (a thickener made with soft butter and flour), which she dissolved in some water taken from the pan the pasta was cooking in. So, you have to cook the pasta, quickly cut the ham into cubes, and then whip up the sauce gently so as to avoid lumps. The right consistency for the sauce – according to the advice of the grandson, who took a while to master this recipe – is pretty liquid, even a bit too liquid, since you are going to add grated gruyère cheese. Yes, gruyère with a small G: it no longer comes just from Switzerland: they make in Finland, for one.

© belgiumtheplaceto.be TM - J Jeanmart

Whatever, as long as it makes strings when it melts! The final touch comes from adding a pinch of grated nutmeg. You can make this with just about any kind of pasta. Better than marcaroni perhaps are *fusilli* or *spirale,* as they hold the sauce better. You can add cream too, if you really want to splash out.

Les crêpes and les "bouquêtes"

© belgiumtheplaceto.be TM - J Jeanmart

OK, so crêpes (thin pancakes, in case you are wondering) are not specifically Belgian. Our neighbours eat them too – north, south, east and west. But in Belgium they have a special status.

First of all, for one day a year they serve as a weather barometer – usurping the role of the frog, our traditional symbol of weather forecasting. At the festival of Candlemas (Chandeleur) on 2 February we say: *'À la Chandeleur, l'hiver se meurt ou reprend vigueur,'* i.e. winter is either about to end, or take a turn for the worse. Time to make some pancakes, because on that day if you toss pancakes with your right hand while holding a gold coin in your left, the year will turn out well for you. And, my goodness, the Belgians sure know how to toss a pancake. Take the example of Gaston Lagaffe, the accident-prone comic-strip character by André Franquin: he sticks them to the ceiling – the ambition of every hotel-and-catering student throughout the kingdom. Our crêpes may not have the distinction of the *crêpe bretonne* (from Brittany) made with buckwheat flour, or the generous scale of the *crêpe normande* (from Normandy), served with flambéed apples, nor even the luxurious thickness of American-style pancakes and drop scones, fattened by a raising agent – unless you're talking Bouquettes (see below). No, we do crêpes unplugged, the straight deal, ready to turn any which way you want to take them: naughty but nice when packed with *cassonade* (fine granulated sugar, *blonde* or *brune,* as your fancy takes you; see page 112); or childhood-revisited when loaded with jam, especially when it gets smeared all over your cheeks during those long, breezy summer days on the coast.

Piled up in a stack, crêpes can become a kind of cake. Here's a simple recipe. You make your crêpes in the classic way, as thin as you can, and then as you stack them you sprinkle each layer generously with *cassonade brune* and small dabs of butter. Little by little, the warmth makes the butter and sugar melt, creating a kind of syrup. When you have finished cooking the crêpes, you just have to cut into the pile like a cake. Sure, it's not exactly delicate, but no one has yet found a better antidote to those days when horizontal rain beats against the windows.

Bouquettes (boûkètes) liégeoises

500g buckwheat flour (called boûkète in the Wallon of Liège), 75g fresh yeast, 2 or 3 eggs, 50cl milk, 50cl water, 5cl rum, 50g raisins (optional), 50g fine sugar, cooking fat (traditionally a mixture of butter and lard). To serve: cassonade (fine granulated sugar) or powder sugar

These leavened buckwheat pancakes are a speciality of Liège, a popular treat traditionally associated with Christmas, and with the '15 Août en Républicue Libre d' Outremeuse', the great festival held on 15 August in the lively 'free republic' of the suburb of Outremeuse. They are usually served with a sprinkling of sugar, or maybe with some Sirop de Liège (see page 131), Nutella even (why not?), and in summer with seasonal fruits.

Les galettes

For readers not familiar with them, *galettes wallonnes* are a small kind of waffle, but thinner and more crisp, and traditionally associated with New Year. In the past they were made in a cast-iron mould, similar to a waffle iron.

This is a story about a great-grandmother and New Year's Day. About the smell of the cold butter-based batter that filled her house during the week that preceded New Year. She spared no effort, and it needed plenty, and pounds of butter, to accomplish her task. Even though she was no longer as willowy and graceful as she once was, her hands exhibited an undiminished skill when it came to turning the iron on the stove.

She made her *galettes* paper-thin. And she stored them delicately in big tins printed with images of the royal family, which she placed in the cupboard of the sideboard in the dining room. On the great day itself she would be ready at first light. She would exchange her checked apron for a pretty floral blouse adorned with her best cameo brooch. A tortoise-shell comb held her tightly knotted bun to the nape of her neck. Now the procession could begin: children, grandchildren, great-grandchildren. Everyone came to wish her a Happy New Year.

And she, light as air and as full of talk as an election night, removed tin after tin from the oak sideboard. They were always the same, her *galettes*, always divinely toothsome. At the start of the day there would be coffee, strong and sweet, as our family likes to drink it. At the end of the day a drop of alcohol in a glass the size of a thimble. We left with our *dringuelle* (a little gift of money), often smiling at how our modern gift to her – usually some kind of electrical gadget for the kitchen – had only half pleased her. For her *galettes*, for her energy, and those New Year's Days that would end in a state of satisfied exhaustion, wherever she now may be: our eternal thanks.

© belgiumtheplaceto.be TM - J Jeanmart

Onion soup –
la soupe à l'oignon

A few winters ago, I went to a Christmas Market, something that I hadn't done for at least two decades. It was almost by chance that I found myself wandering there with some friends, between the rows of prefabricated stalls, immersed in the Christmas carols crackling from poorly adjusted loudspeakers. We had been to a dance show in which a friend of ours had been taking part. A beautiful show, although a bit too long for my bladder and my stomach. My day at work had also been long, and once the dancing was over, I wanted only one thing: to get home and go to sleep. When I received a telephone call cancelling an event that I was really looking forward to, my mood took a turn for the worse. Clearly I had little left to offer the evening, now stripped of that sparkling sense of humour and legendary verve which are the makings of my inestimable charm.

It was misty, chilly, and, as one might expect, there was not a snowflake in sight to brighten the night. All around sellers of foodstuffs presented their wares, some tawdry, some divine. Very quickly the others turned their attention towards plates of half a dozen oysters presented with a glass of champagne. I wasn't in the mood. Close by, however, was a big, boiling casserole. I hesitated, but suddenly my mouth was watering in a way that I could not ignore. *Soupe à l'oignon*, piping hot. It was served in polystyrene cups that were just thick enough to warm your fingers without burning them. The generous mass of cheese and croutons that Madame added suggested that it was better to slide it whole into my mouth to avoid embarrassing myself with a net of stringy cheese

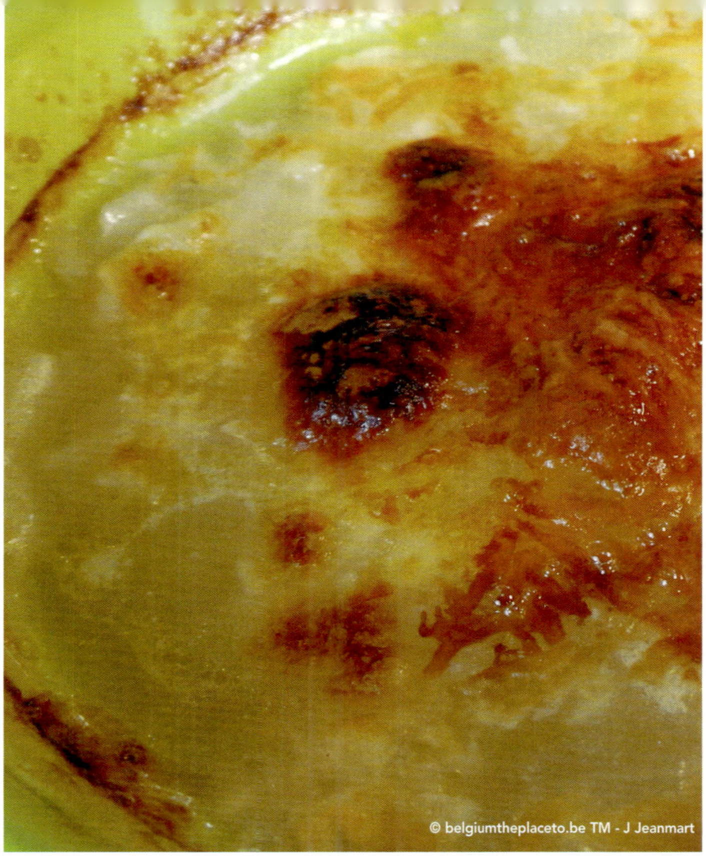
© belgiumtheplaceto.be TM - J Jeanmart

all over my lips. It was like the soup of my memories, packed with onions and with a flavour to match. Not one of those clear, soulless soups. A soup like the ones my dad used to make when I was a child, laying into several kilos of onions as if his life depended on it. Thus it was with a bright and joyful face that I returned to my oyster-eaters. Which all goes to show that I'm not really neurotic – no, not I.

Soupe à l'oignon, that's my kind of Belgian food. It's surely the case for most Belgians too. They all know what it's like to blow in vain across the surface of the bowl, all the while knowing that, out of greedy impatience, they are going to drink it too hot and sacrifice a few taste buds in the process.

Le pain de viandes

Pain de viandes – sounds so much more refined than 'meat loaf', doesn't it? But it's about as straight a translation as you get in the world of culinary terms. That's what we are talking about here: meatloaf. And we Belgians do it especially well. But here's a thing that always makes me laugh: that meatloaf you find in supermarkets called such things as *pain de viande à l'ancienne* (old-fashioned style) or *pain de viande maison* (home-cooked style). OK, so maybe it will be good, perhaps the meat will be fresh and of good quality, but – blistering barnacles! – meatloaf is a thing that simply has to be home-made! There are no two ways about it.

The essential building block is mince. In French this is called *haché or hachis,* and I'm going to digress to explain the difference, so you don't die in ignorance. *Haché* is a contraction of the term *viande hachée,* meaning minced meat (note how it also contracts in the heat of your oven). By contrast, *hachis,* – a term used wrongly by butchers who have not yet read these words – is a preparation made using *haché,* the most famous of which is called *hachis Parmentier,* a refined form of cottage or shepherd's pie. You should also know that you can mince anything you like in the animal or vegetable kingdom to make *haché.* In general we Belgians like to mince beef, veal and pork (albeit that the latter is off the agenda for certain religions), but in other countries, even continents, goat and lamb may also get a look in.

Once you've brought your minced meat, all you need is a few stale loaf-ends of bread. Normally if you haven't gone overboard with the French toast (*pain perdu,* see page 117), there'll be some lurking in the bread bin. You soak the bread in a well-judged mixture of milk, egg yoke, salt, pepper, herbs and spices. Once soggy, mash the bread up with the meat and then shape the aforementioned

meatloaf with your hands. If you are married, don't forget to remove your wedding ring, for fear of losing it in the mixture, which can have ugly consequences, particularly if your other half breaks a tooth on it. Then pop it in the oven. A good hour per kilo at 200°C should do the trick – just enough time to mow the lawn. What's not to like?

Chervil soup – *la soupe au cerfeuil*

I know, chervil soup, *la soupe au cerfeuil,* is not really Belgian as such, I agree; it's just a deep, nostalgic longing for it that pierces my soul – like what the Portuguese call *saudade,* and sing about in their heartbreaking *fado*. For chervil soup is really the taste of tastes to me – a whole album of images, of memories.

At the entrance to Plasstraat, coming from the motorway, there was a small hillock. Then one or two bends, and in the middle of the hedge, on the right, the gate to my grandmother's property. It was a bit of a mess of greenery, with big trees, a nonchalantly untrimmed hedge, an old sand pit long abandoned to weeds. The laurel arbour had been the setting for countless bed-sheet cabins and – even then – feasts. She is standing at her window, a reflection of sunlight preventing me seeing her smile, but I see her hand waving to me. I walk up the wooden steps to a terrace and wall covered in cement tiles. Behind the first window hangs a panel, its lettering, in English, faded by time and weather: Fun House. Above the double door, which would be thrown open in full summer, there was a medallion bearing the profile of someone whose name I have forgotten. The toy box stood like a counter on the left. I walk past the wood-fired heating stove, the one-legged milking stool and the halberd. The clock on the dresser has not worked for years. She is there, in her minuscule kitchen. On one side, cupboards with two-coloured sliding doors, on the other her cooker and a traditional soup-stove or *potager.* On this her green enamel casserole takes pride of place. She greets me with *'Bonjour mon petit coco'*. Although she was no more than 1m 60cm (5ft 3in) tall, I was always her *'petit coco'* (little darling, pet). There was nothing out of the ordinary about her: she was a grandmother like perhaps there are not enough of, and I cherish deeply my memories of her. But what I can't for the life of me recall is the flavour of that soup. I can remember its texture, its smell, but not the taste. The smell, when it comes back to me, makes me think of parsley cut with scissors in a glass. Something green, fresh, straight from the garden. I think she put in a few potatoes to give the soup some body. To accompany it, I remember slices of bread which she cut with a strange knife, shaped like a bow-saw. She signed a cross before attacking it, then cut off the slices. She spread hers with Planta margarine because she had to be a bit careful, then we could tuck in. Happily, after her, the cottage was destroyed. Not a single trace of it remains; as a result my memories are not mixed with the present, and it is better like that. Memories are part of us, and sometimes offer us a refuge in some other place which will never again exist.

Apple tart –
la tarte aux pommes

Belgian pâtisserie, and especially the tarts, is almost as celebrated as our famous *frites*. In fact, there are more sorts of tarts in Belgium than types of sauce in a *frites* stall – and that's saying something!

But, while apple tart *(la tarte aux pommes)* has played a part in the Belgian food landscape for as long as our orchards have groaned with the weight of fruit and our cows have produced milk, our hens eggs, and our fields wheat – our fine country cannot lay any claim to its invention.

People eat apple tart just about everywhere in Europe and North America. If Africa and Asia don't go in for it in a big way, that's their hard luck. All this is a way of saying that, if our apple tart is the best, it's because it the best according to our tastes. Tastes which we have nurtured on our tongues since infancy. You will believe me, no doubt, when I say that we consistently underestimate the power of our memory for tastes, and even more so our memory of smell.

I know, for instance, that we can be led blindfolded into some place of our early childhood, where there is nothing to recognise it apart from the smell, and that this smell alone will allow you to identify the place. For me, I know this because that would work for a kitchen of my childhood. I left that remark in the conditional because that kitchen now exists only in my memories. Apple peel – broken into pieces, because I had had little practice in wielding the little knife. Dough left to rise under a kitchen cloth in the front room, which was warmed by the sun at the start of the afternoon. Its smell when it was under the rolling pin. It wasn't a wooden rolling pin, but a wine bottle, the label from which had long since disappeared. Flour coating the vinyl surface as well as the bottle. The apple quarters were ready. I had already pinched plenty of pieces before snaffling up the survivors with a fork and arranging them in a spiral curling in

© belgiumtheplaceto.be TM - J Jeanmart

towards the centre of the tart. A few holes in the crust, that made it prettier. We had an old black baking tin. It made the best tarts, with a fine and soft pastry. That's also because we didn't skimp on the butter.

Butter in little lumps dotting the apples. Fine sugar sprinkled over the top, and then it was the turn of the oven. In my home sometimes we covered the apples with *crème anglaise* (a sophisticated form of custard). That gave them a different kind of crunchiness. But uncovered and delicately caramelised, that pleased me just as much. Memories, huh?

Sweetened condensed milk – Le lait condensé sucré

So, for the photo we looked everywhere for a tin of Petite Hollandaise. Arghhh! Where are the police when you need them? Quick, let's put up posters everywhere in the street, giving my telephone number to one and all – I want news! What has happened to Petite Hollandaise? I knew her so well, that little Dutch girl. She had a little cloth bonnet, a blue-striped dress, clogs and nice red cheeks. In the background there was a windmill, Delft-style. My Petite Hollandaise lived at my uncle's. Well it seemed a bit like that. The Café Chez Mon Oncle doubled up as a small grocery. It was run by Marie, who was married to Yvon, but he wasn't really my uncle, and Marie was not my aunt. But close enough as not to matter. Well, you might find this confusing if you didn't know my village of Grandrieu, right by the French border, before about twenty years ago. It's your loss.

The Café Chez Mon Oncle stood opposite the church; at that time, when people went to Mass every Sunday, there had to be a café opposite the church. Yvon ruled from the bar and the main attraction for me was the table football game that stood right beside it. Marie ran the grocery, sometimes with her daughter. Whenever we needed something at home – some salt, matches, whatever – my brother or I were given the job of going to Marie. Me, on my bike, ecstatic with joy. My Petite Hollandaise lived on the shelf just behind Marie. With the shopping money, I would buy myself a small tin of this sweetened condensed milk. She was on the label, looking at me with her little mocking smile, as if saying: 'Come on old chap, I know you love me, but stop it. This just won't work out. And besides, you've got a double chin already.' Later condensed milk came in tubes, but the taste was never quite the same. Even so, when the tube was almost empty, you would still stick in the tip of your tongue to suck out the very last drop.

© belgiumtheplaceto.be TM - Eric Boschman

Les tartines russes

Tartine usually means a slice of bread slathered with butter, ready to receive a thick layer of jam or *cassonade* (sugar). Or, by extension a sandwich. That's the reference here: a pair of biscuits sandwiching a creamed butter filling. Noone knows quite where these biscuity wonders came from originally, but the clue could be in the name. And if not Russia, then at least somewhere far north, to judge by the large quantity of butter involved – a well-known antidote to the cold. Children love them – love to eat them, love to make them. They are the stuff of childhood, and childhood memories, and bring out the child in everyone.

FROM RUSSIA WITH LOVE (for 6 people)
For the biscuits: 100g butter, 100g cassonade (golden, granulated sugar); 100g flour. For the filling: 3 eggs, 150g sugar, 250g butter

For the biscuits: In a bowl, work the butter until soft, add the sugar and then the flour to make a dough. When consistent, make it into a brick-shape, then wrap it in cling film and refrigerate for 30 minutes. Heat the oven to 180°C. Slice the dough brick thinly, tidy up and roll if necessary to make neat, even rectangles, then place the slices on a baking paper on a baking tray, and bake until brown (8–10 minutes). Remove from the oven to cool and harden.

For the filling: Make a *bain marie* with boiling water, then break the eggs into a bowl over the *bain marie,* add the sugar and blend while it warms, until the mixture is pale yellow and creamy. Off the heat, add the butter in small dice to create a smooth cream. Allow to cool.

Assembly: take a pair of biscuits; spread the filling on the lower one, and press the second on top. Refrigerate in order to serve very cold.

© Boulangerie Vienne

© belgiumtheplaceto.be TM - J Jeanmart

11. (literally) Cheesy food

Bâtards, pistolets and other breads

'As long as there is bread on the table, there is hope,' goes the old saying. And Belgium, buffeted over the centuries by invaders from all parts of Europe, should indeed have deep resources of hope to drawn on. Bakers produce loafs of all shapes and sizes – white, brown, rye, wholewheat, seeded, sourdough, with raisins, with lumps of sugar and salt. Alain Coumont, the Walloon founder or the Brussels-based, now international, chain of bakery-restaurants called Le Pain Quotidien ('The Daily Bread'), was inspired by the varieties of bread that he saw his Ardennaise grandmother make, as he stood on a chair to watch, and his mission has been to revive and preserve those traditions. If you are looking to see what Belgian bread looks like, Le Pain Quotidien is a good place to start.

The names can be a bit alarming. The blameless *bâtard* (literally, bastard) is a loaf of about 500g that was born of an illicit union between a baguette and a 1kg loaf, and bears a tell-tale resemblance to both. *Pistolet* means 'pistol': where on earth did this crusty round bread roll – so beloved in Belgium – get that name? Pistols at dawn? Well, not quite – but many Belgians see the *pistolet* uniquely in the context of Sunday morning, with the newspaper, slippers, dressing gown, embattled hair, children zapping cartoons on TV. For others, *pistolets* can feature any day of the week. Prepared like a sandwich, prior to the advent of the demi-baguette it was the kind of snack you found at a butcher's, filled with ham or *filet américain*. Some people just pick out the white crumb; others remove that and just eat the crust. Kept whole, cut in two, it is usually pasted with a prodigious quantity of butter. *Pistolets* don't usually end up in children's school lunchboxes because they have the annoying habit of going soft: best eaten fresh, straight from the baker's, where they will have been baked that very morning. With butter and pieces of ham in the first, cheese in the second, jam in the third – and, for some lucky folk heading towards lunchtime, stuffed with brown shrimps whilst gazing out over the North Sea. Now that's a real joy!!

There's also a good line in sugared breads too, such as *craquelin*. In its original Dutch form, *"craquelink"* was a little dry biscuit, but in Belgium it became soft, sweet bread, sparkling with a generous sprinkling of pearl sugar felicitously resisting the bite – its name is like the sound that goes off in your head when you eat it. To revive one's spirits on a cold winter morning, after three days of rain, there's nothing like a nice slice of *craquelin*, thickly spread with butter, and dipped into a cup of good hot chocolate.

Another one to look out for – similarly covered with little sugar diamonds, but crisper and flavoured with cinnamon – is the Bruxellois speciality *pain à la grecque*. Greek you might think, to judge by the name. No, actually: the name is a corruption of the *gracht* part of Wolvensgrachtstraat (Rue Fossé-aux-Loups), in central Brussels, home to a religious order that first made this bread in the 16th century. You can still buy it at the fabulous Biscuiterie Dandoy, just a few hundred metres away. A real taste of local history!

La maquée

A nice big slice of bread spread with salted butter, covered with a good centimetre of *fromage blanc,* sprinkled with salt and pepper and chopped chives, with thin, round slices of radish from the garden… it's the classic accompaniment for beer, the sort of thing you find in a fine old, time-honoured *estaminet* (tavern). And it's even better when, instead of standard *fromage blanc,* you use *maquée.*

To make your own *maquée,* it's best to have a farm within milk-can carrying distance. Plus muslin and rennet. What really matters above all is that the milk has to be fresh. If it's been processed by bactofugation, that's OK, but you can't used industrialised, carton milk: it's been treated too much and won't curdle. Some years ago, when I was very small, my mother decided to make *maquée* herself. A good city girl freshly arrived in the countryside, she wanted to be as self-sufficient as she could be. We did at least stop at having cows in the garden, but that's about all we were spared. Fetching milk was one of the jobs my brother and I were landed with. We had to cross the road, milk-can in hand, go into the cowshed, and walk between the two rows of hairy, farting, shitting monsters, in order to find Madame Huart. She always smiled at us as she got up from her stool on which she sat to reach the plump udders of the cows. She walked a few metres, her rubber boots never slipping on the slimy stuff that covered the concrete in the middle. She took a large metal jug and poured enough to fill our can. And so back to the house with our precious cargo slopping about in all directions.

Coming out of the cowshed, especially in winter, meant a blast of cold, a bit like a slap in the face to wake you up. Back home, the milk was boiled. Ugh, that skin on the surface, how I hated that! Then part of it was used to make *maquée,* and the rest was set aside

© belgiumtheplaceto.be TM - J Jeanmart

for us. It's strange that only now do I realise that this stuff is rather good. At the time it was more of a boring, idiotic chore that we were forced to partake in when the weather was bad outside. A few years later, long after my mother had lost her passion for local produce, I discovered that someone was making a goat *maquée* in the village. My parents served it in the restaurant accompanied by liquid honey. Catalan-style. Oh, how I could gorge myself on that stuff! What a supreme balance of flavours! The art of preparation consisted simply of conscientiously mashing the cheese with enough honey to make a thick syrup. Bliss, I tell you – pure bliss.

Le fromage de Herve

'Herve, une saveur d'avance.' That was the slogan chosen by the tourist office for this town in the Province of Liège. Nice in French: impossible in English. It's a play on the slogan of the Province of Luxembourg: *'Une ardeur d'avance'*, which means something like 'Ahead with enthusiasm.' But in Herve *ardeur* has been replaced by *saveur,* one of those French words, like *terroir,* that refuses translation: 'flavour' is a bit vapid. 'Herve, ahead in flavour'? Well, certainly the fame of Herve cheese goes before it – not to mention its pungent smell. It's the only cheese in Belgium that has been granted brand protection under AOP status *(Appellation d'Origine Protégée)*. That means the EU has taken the matter seriously and laid down a series of criteria that the cheese must meet regarding the geographical limits of production, the way the cattle are fed, how they are milked, the method used to curdle the milk and to make and mature the cheese, and so on, thanks to which, when you buy a Herve cheese, you know what you are buying and are not swindled.

The history of the individual cheeses – for there are a number of varieties – is well documented and dates back almost eight centuries. They were already making cheese on the Herve plateau in the 13th century. It is now made by the Fromagerie Herve Société. It's a soft, washed-rind cheese, made with pasteurised or unpasteurised cow's milk. The internal structure of the cheese is consistent, firm, creamy and has a 45% minimum fat content. Herve Remoudou is the top dog. It's a farmhouse Herve made with unpasteurised milk, matured for two to three months, which lends it its frank and assertive character. It's the end-of-meal cheese *par excellence,* with a strong aroma. *Herve doux* (mild) and *Herve piquant* (strong) are made with pasteurised milk. They are matured for 4–6 and 5–7 weeks respectively.

© OPT-Avantage

Now that you know a little more about these cheeses, dear seekers of true taste and flavour, make an excursion to the green meadows of the Herve plateau. Go and taste the cheese on the spot. Presented on a slice of bread and butter, perhaps also spread with a thin layer of Sirop de Liège (see page 131), to be dunked in black coffee, the *saveur* will never be better, and you will understand why it is ahead of the game – and *une saveur d'avance* will need no further translation.

Le sirop de Liège

Here's another nice slice of history which, give or take a bit, is almost as old as Belgium itself. I'm exaggerating a little, but even so, this history does go back to 1902, the date when the idea of making a fruity commercial product from Belgium's juice-laden orchards formed in the head of Clément I. No, this wasn't the pope, but a man with small glasses and good business nous: Clément Meurens, founder of a dynasty of syrup-makers. He decided to build his *siroperie* in Aubel near the railway station, with the dream of distributing his 'Sirop de Liège' around the planet. And it worked! Because the whole world wants vitamins, and the ability to give themselves brown moustaches, and to have sticky fingers for life – and not everyone had access to pears, a press and a copper boiler suitable for steam-cooking. For that is what it is: a delicious jammy paste, made of concentrated pears, plus apples, plums and apricots.

I won't give all the details of the story of the Cléments, but under Clément II the slogan *'Du Vrai Sirop de Liège'* ('True' or 'Authentic' Liège Syrup) first appeared on its cardboard containers. Along with the white pear trees on a background of green meadows beneath a blue sky, forming a frieze around the containers. Simple and timeless.

That was 1947, so for more than half a century now this image has been a part of our visual landscape of taste.

Sirop de Liège has a variety of uses: on toast and slices of bread at breakfast and as a late-night snack, at teatime, as an ingredient for *Boulets sauce lapin* (see page 154) and glazed pork ribs, for Camembert or Herve toasts melted on the barbecue then grilled with a thick layer of *sirop* on top, and for gluing football stickers into Panini albums. This list is by no means exhaustive. Essentially, Belgium would not really be Belgium if it didn't guiltily dip the tip of a knife into a pot of *Vrai Sirop de Liège* for a last taste before closing it.

© belgiumtheplaceto.be TM - J Jeanmart

Le Choco Prince

Ah, now here's a biscuit for children, if ever there was one. A sandwich of two glazed and crisp slices of *sablé* biscuit filled with soft and creamy chocolate. Just look at the dashing Prince Charming on the packet, inviting you into his dreams, goading you into pulling the biscuits apart in order to lick the chocolate inside.

He's older than he looks. Choco Prince first appeared in 1926, made by De Beukelaar of Antwerp. In 1980 he married into the royal French line of LU, which is now part of the glorious empire of Kraft. No matter: despite his elevation to the world stage, noone has forgotten that he is of Belgian stock, through and through, least of all the Belgians, and that he has a special bond with the children of his homeland.

For some years now, there's been a form of Choco Prince with a white chocolate filling. This came as a bit of a shock to me. I mean, really, who could possibly like white Choco Princes? They'll try anything. Why not multi-grain, diet Choco Princes while we are at it? OK, I confess, I have experimented with the white filling and, honestly, it has not nearly the same creaminess. It just seems, well... short on the chocolate. That's the long and short of it.

Personally, what I really like is the corrugated cardboard tube which tears rather badly bit by bit as one eats through the packet. Then, best of all, are the fragments in the bottom that you nibble in order not to waste a single crumb. By the way, there is perhaps a good business waiting to be created there: broken fragments of *marrons glacés* are packaged and sold, so why not the crumbs from tubes of Choco Prince?

Choco Prince can also be found these days in individual 'Prince Pockets', in twos. But two little disks of Prince, that's just too little. You have to agree.

© belgiumtheplaceto.be TM - J Jeanmart

Le fromage en cubes au sel de céleri

In Belgium, apératifs – or *'l'apéro'* – tend to turn into a feast and are often more focused on the eats than the drinks. With us, you don't get just an olive or two with your Pastis, so this puts you under an obligation to drink a dozen glasses simply to assist you in digesting all you have to eat.

We love paprika-flavoured crisps, thick slices of sausage and salami (bits of which always get stuck in your teeth), crunchy gherkins, salted biscuits in the shape of fish and, of course, cubes of cheese.

It does not really matter what sort of cheese: any kind of hardish cheese hanging about in your fridge will do the trick. But for this purpose definitely avoid soft cheeses like *maquée* (see page 129), goat, camembert, and triangles of Vache Qui Rit, none of which match the required qualification of being cubic or suitable for skewering with a toothpick.

The absolute best thing to have – *le top du top*, as they say in such circles – on the low table of the living room is a giant serving plate loaded with cheese cubes with a colour-range from the off-white of Maredsous to the orange of Mimolette.

Celery salt is the inseparable friend of *l'apéro*. It provides precious assistance to the managers of our nation's innumerable bars, nudging clients towards a second glass by creating the illusion that this will quench the thirst provoked by the excess of salt.

Originally celery salt was made from celery seeds. Aphrodisiac properties were attributed to these seeds, based on the popular belief that the plant came under the influence of the moon and its ancient Greek goddess Selene, from whom the name was said to be derived. And as we know, nothing can resist the moon, not even the frostiest young lady sitting neatly on the edge of the sofa, skirt tightly pulled over her resolutely clenched knees. These days celery salt more often comes from a mix of salt and powdered celeriac root, which is easier to process than the seeds.

© OPT-Avantage

But in the end, the type of celery salt matters as little as the type of cheese. Sprinkle the former over the latter, roll the six sides of the cubes in the powder, use a finger to casually pick up the loose grains scattered around the edge of a plate, but whatever you do, don't sell your pleasure short. Pleasure is what you make of it, and it's even better with celery salt.

The Flagey Building
© belgiumtheplaceto.be TM - J Jeanmart

12. F(l)ood The alcoholic ones:

La Leffe

Leffe is one of the best known of the 'abbey beers'. It is now brewed and sold by AB InBev (the multinational conglomerate headquartered in Leuven, Belgium, makers of Stella Artois), and is no longer produced at the charming little abbey in Wallonia beside the River Meuse where it originated, and whose name it still carries – and which still receives a royalty for the recipe.

Leffe enjoyed such an outstanding commercial success over the past few decades that, in 1994, it developed the concept of the 'Café Leffe'. This started with cafés situated in the centre of 13 tourist-destination towns such as Dinant (hometown of Leffe), Brussels, Bruges, Ghent and Charleroi. Next, the Cafés Leffe launched an assault on the main capital cities of the world at large.

In a Café Leffe, you drink Leffe beer, of course. In all its forms: *blonde, brune* (brown), *triple* (strong, 8.5% ABV) and *radieuse* (literally, 'radiant': amber-dark, 8.2% ABV), and served at the perfect temperature in the appropriate glass with maybe a bit of cheese on the side. The décor of the cafés goes with the product, i.e. in

© belgiumtheplaceto.be TM - J Jeanmart

harmony with the simplicity of monastic life, but without the church services. I don't know if grace is supposed to be said here before a meal, but if not, at least it might be worth giving the idea some thought. Leffe's commercial initiatives did not stop there – that would have been a pity with such as great beer. The food served is in on the act: *Carbonnades flamandes à la Leffe brune* (sweetened beef stew cooked in brown Leffe), quiche made with *radieuse, Poularde à la branbançonne à la triple* (fattened chicken cooked with caramelised endives in Leffe *triple*) – so many good reasons to steer clear of that lean-ham and low-fat cheese salad.

Le Pékèt

What else would you expect from the people of Liège when one knows about the birth of their mythical, devil-may-care folk-hero and mascot Tchantchès? On 25 August AD 760 the popular quarter called Outremeuse – or Djus d'la Moûse, in local parlance – witnessed the birth of this baby. Chubby-cheeked and strong, he smiled at one and all. Suddenly he began to sing *"Allons la mère Gaspard, encore un verre, encore un verre!"* ("Come on Mother Gaspard, another glass, another glass!") Some good woman rushed to him with a glass of water. The baby pushed it away and began to sulk. The husband of this good woman instead offered him a biscuit dipped in *pékèt* (a local version of *jenever* gin, flavoured with juniper berries, usually drunk neat), which the baby consumed greedily, promptly demanding more. So he was given a bottle of this precious distillate, and he took a big swig as if it was milk. The good woman and her husband adopted the child and named him Tchantchès – that's François in Walloon. Nourished primarily by *pékèt*, the child grew like a mushroom. Once his adoptive father had the misguided idea to give him a *hareng saur* (a kind of kippered herring), which he much enjoyed. But the salt in it inflamed his gullet – so it was back to the biscuits dipped in *pékèt*. As he got older, his parents noticed that his nose was growing disproportionately fast. Contrary to what you might think, this peculiarity was not due to the *pékèt*, but to an accident that occurred at his christening. The midwife who was carrying him also liked a drink. That day she must have drunk more than her normal dose, because she left Tchantchès in the font. The child unfortunately bumped his nose on the holy stone. Being made of stern stuff, he did not cry, but the excessive growth of his nose resulted from this trauma. He also suffered another misfortune: he contracted measles. At this time, the way to cure this disease was to drink iron-rich water – also recommended as a cure for alcoholism, as it happens. His mother made some by putting a horseshoe in a bucket of water. Because he hated water, he drank the entire bucket all at once, and the horseshoe got stuck in his throat. No one could dislodge it. From that day on he was unable to turn his head sideways. Saddled with these two disfigurements, he became the butt of jokes and sarcastic remarks. What's more, his skin was strangely coloured: ruddy, with splashes of purple and violet. Very soon his face became the model for carnival masks. Nonetheless, on the eve of Assumption in AD 770 he was elected Prince of Djus d'la Moûse. On that day he came to the realisation that ugliness, if accompanied by generosity of spirit, is no barrier to affection.

During the Fêtes de Wallonie, held each year in September, one hears talk of a 'Route de Pékèt', but unfortunately no-one who has participated has ever been able to give us a precise account of the itinerary. But despair not! You can drink the best Pékèt in Liège at the aptly-named Maison du Pékèt.

La Lambic

If there are any causes worth fighting for, here is one. *Lambic* beer is unique in the world. And the main reason for this lies in the unique way it is made. This is brewing at its most authentic, primordial.

Water, the purest possible, malted barley and hops. Nothing else. The brewer makes a judicious mix of these ingredients and boils them up. If you have the good fortune to witness the brewing, and to share breakfast with the brewer, you can – if you are very good – get to taste the nascent brew. It is soft, sweet, and has a smell reminiscent of Ovaltine ('Ovomaltine' to the Belgians). Once the brew is sufficiently reduced – for it's this reduction that's important, in order to concentrate the sugars that have naturally accumulated in the malt – the next stage is the cooling. And it is precisely here that the miracle occurs. The embryonic *lambic* is sent to cool in large, open-topped copper vats and exposed to the air. Shhh! Don't say anything! This is of course done beneath the shelter of a roof, because, given our national climate, if you did this without a roof you'd end up with a thin barley soup, with no approximation to the divine beverage intended. Here, in the open air, the liquid is exposed to contamination by airborne yeasts. Horror! Scandal! You want us to drink stuff full of air pollution? Yessiree! Because this is good pollution. The yeasts even have pretty names: *Brettanomyces bruxellensis* or *lambicus*. By a stroke of luck, they are found naturally only in the valley of the River Senne, which flows, largely hidden, through Brussels and the Pajottenland to the west of Brussels – the homelands of *lambic,* and through the Walloon Brabant. That is why *lambic* is unique in the world and can be made only in Brussels and to the west of the city.

About three days after the contamination, the fermentation begins. This is followed by maturation in oak barrels for a year or more.

© belgiumtheplaceto.be TM - J Jeanmart

At around 5.5% ABV, it has a distinctive, slightly winey flavour. *Lambic* is also the mother of *kriek* and *gueuze* – two other Brussels specialities. You've got to try some: you haven't really been to Brussels unless you do. Better still, visit the Cantillon brewery in the western suburb of Anderlecht to witness at first hand why this is a cause worth fighting for.

La Kriek

© belgiumtheplaceto.be TM - Eric Boschman

It's almost an onomatopoeia. A bit like the noise made by a cellar door opened a bit too quickly, or perhaps the sound of a cherry stone being crushed. And the cherry stone has some bearing on this story. *Kriek* means 'cherry' in Dutch and in Bruxellois (the dialect of Brussels). By extension, it's the name of a beer made with cherries. Special cherries are used: not the sweet and juicy *bigarreau* eating cherries – the kind that children love to crush onto their new white T-shirts just as you've run out of Persil Non-Bio. No, *kriek* is made from Schaerbeek cherries – sour Morello cherries closely related to wild cherries, and traditionally produced in the Brussels suburb of Schaerbeek.

They have big stones, and not much flesh and above all a sourness that discourages the crows. This means they can be picked before the birds feast on them and placed in barrels of *lambic* (see above). Traditionally 650-litre port 'pipes' (barrels) are used, so 150kg of cherries is put into 500 litres of one-and-a-half-year-old *lambic*. And that's just about it. Yeasts attached to the skins of the fruit, airborne yeasts in the cellar and the sugars contained in the juice as well as in the *lambic* come together in one big party. The pipe begins to foam; after five days it's away.

It takes a few weeks for the alcohol in the beer to extract the colour particles contained in the skin and the flesh of the fruit. It's from this that *kriek lambic* (to give the finished product its full name) acquires its wonderful deep ruby colour. After this, it's all a question of taste. Aficionados of this great Brabant treasure like it as natural and authentic as possible, even if it means dissolving a lump of sugar in it to reduce the sourness. They dismiss the more commercial brands of *kriek* as over-sugared, over-coloured and over-perfumed.

Similar methods are used to make *lambic* into *framboise* (flavoured with raspberries) and *faro* (flavoured with sugar and caramel), both definitely worth exploration, and better than they may sound.

But *kriek* is my first love. *Kriek*, it's the noise my grandmother's green cellar door made whenever I opened it surreptitiously to play doctors and nurses with the neighbour's daughter among the bottles of *gueuze* and *kriek* marked simply with a spot of white paint. Ah, the sweet, effervescent associations of youth!

La Gueuze

Gueuze, gueuse: now there's a word with a colourful past! It can mean a block of 'pig' (i.e. crude) lead, or a woman of dodgy morals, or the wife of a *gueux*, a beggar – a term that was also attached to a band of heroic swashbuckling anti-Spanish nobles in 16th-century Netherlands. Maybe *gueuze* was the favourite drink of those heroic Gueux; it wouldn't surprise me. Anyhow, she is the daughter of Lambic, but not of Sidonie! And there you have a truly Belgian joke, which you won't understand unless you are familiar (a) with the Bruxellois beer called *lambic* (see above), and (b) the classic Belgian cartoon strip *Bob et Bobette* (*Suske en Wiske* in Dutch, *Spike and Suzy* in Britain, and *Willy and Wanda* in the US). Lambique is a prominent character in the stories, so… oh, hang it!

'So how is *gueuze* made?' I asked Jean-Pierre Van Roy one day at the Cantillon brewery in Brussels. 'With love and a bit of patience,' he replied. Well, I knew already that love demands a lot of patience; and I had a suspicion that *gueuze* required the same.

Gueuze is a bit like the champagne of beer. The miracle behind it is the bottling together of two *lambic* beers, one young, one old. The young still contains actively fermenting ingredients, the old some ingredients that offer themselves up as the target of additional fermentation. The two, both crying out for this clinch of fermentation, are sealed into a bottle. It's fiesta-time in there, as the natural yeasts of the *lambic* do the conga with the natural sugars. And go for it I say: the outcome is alcohol with a bit of carbonic gas as a by-product. Thus the bubbles are born.

A *gueuze* is a delicate thing, unsweetened, unfiltered, and above all not messed about with to achieve that detestable kind of thick, white head of foam that looks like the iceberg that sank the Titanic and is just about as unsinkable. *Gueuze* is stored in its bottle, sometimes for many years, and when it is not disgorged (separated from the lees), it can – just like its cousin champagne – defy time. There are some happy maniacs who are proud to collect bottles from the best producers, thumb their noses at the passage of time, and from time to time savour an aged *gueuze*. It has just the right amount of bitterness at the back of the mouth to make one regret the loss of youth, but not so much to prevent one appreciating the upsides of ageing.

© belgiumtheplacetobe.be TM - Eric Boschman

La Vieux Temps

Vieux Temps: 'Old Times'. For me, this evokes the café opposite the church, beside the war memorial. A café relatively smoke-free, rare for those days. Table football to the right of the entrance, posters about upcoming dances and other such events next to the door that led to the private part to the left of the bar counter. Yuccas or some other equally resilient indoor plants stood on the windowsills. At the back, a door opened into a grocery shop which – to be a bit more chic and with-it – we called a *'superette'* (i.e. a mini supermarket). The bar was enormously high, or so it seemed at my age. It was permanently occupied by one or two heavyweights with the distant look of the working day behind them. A bar made of red-brown wood, or at least a red-brown wood veneer; it had fluting which hurt my cheeks if I pressed them against it. There was also a jukebox behind the column in a recess, beside the posters. It sparkled and glowed in the half-light of dusk, as it played corny love and pop songs that even at the time seemed dated. As the French pop star couple Sheila and Ringo belted out *Les gondoles à Venise* – disdainfully spurning Venice, the Pyramids and Capri for their happily ordinary love-life at home – I watched the immobile hands of the Stella Artois clock set over the alcove that separated the two main rooms, waiting for the song to end. The chairs – cheap, creaking, unmatching – made a distinctive noise against the tiled floor. The tables had tops covered with formica, or some other similarly shiny substance. The grown-ups nursed glasses of *gueuze* flavoured with grenadine, Chimay or Vieux Temps. Around a tooth stump stuck to a pendulous lower lip, one of these would from time to time mumble something, and another would mutter a reply, punctuated by his cigarette, typically a yellow maize-paper Gitane. When he eventually left and squeezed himself behind the wheel of his car, the headlights lit up in yellow, as French cars did at the time, to head back across the border. On busy days, such as after

© belgiumtheplaceto.be TM - Eric Boschman

mass on Sunday morning, a few couples might come in. He would drink a *'pale-ale'* (a Belgian adoption), and she water. If they both drank, it was because they were not respectable. At the time there was a slogan which amused and perplexed me even then: *'Remontez le temps, descendez un Vieux Temps'*. A loose English equivalent would be 'Wind back time, unwind with a Vieux Temps'.

It reminded me a bit of the wall of my grandmother's toilet: being of artistic bent, she had decorated it with a big collage made up of hundreds of pictures of food and drink, with a caption in the middle written in cut-outs like an anonymous letter: 'All good things come to an end,' it declared.

The brand Vieux Temps still exists today, a malty, complex pale-ale. But the original brewery in Mont-St-Guibert, Walloon Brabant, lives on only in memory. As does the café in the village, and my grandmother's collage. Old times, already.

Le Zizi Coin Coin

Zizi Coin Coin, or more precisely Zizi Coin Coin Lemon Cocktail, may have entered the collective memory of Belgian taste only relatively recently, but we've seen the same phenomenon among our good neighbours in France: this 100% Belgian product has boldly entered the cherished realm of apératif drinks, giving its more traditional rivals a run for their money.

A meticulous survey carried out by the authors of this fine book among a range of loyal Tintin readers has revealed the following fact: in the group aged 7 to 77, 100% knew what Zizi Coin Coin is.

A number of factors account for this. First there was *'La Danse des canards'* ('The Dance of the Ducks', but known as 'The Chicken Dance' in the English-speaking world), the fab mega-hit song of the 1980s by J.-J. Lionel. The chorus in French goes *'Coin-coin, coin-coin'* (quack, quack). Add to this *'Le Zizi'* by Pierre Perret from a few years before, which – with all the no-holds-barred frankness of French song – gives a witty topographical account of *le zizi*, the willy or penis. So 'Willy Quack Quack'. You get the drift. Anyhow, in my humble opinion, these two combined had already subtly prepared the neurones of future consumers by the time of the drink's much trumpeted big launch by a company in Huy, on the River Meuse west of Liège, in 1998.

OK, so the official version is that 'Zi' comes from the zest of lemon and the *coin coin* from the duck. But, you know me: I like to see things in their broader cultural context.

The label on the bottle has the reassuring air of something quite innocent, but when you know that Belgians are capable of eating *pistolets* ('pistols,' see page 128) for breakfast, *boulets* ('cannonballs', see page 154) for lunch, and a *mitraillette*

© belgiumtheplaceto.be TM - J Jeanmart

('machinegun', see page 82) for supper, you see how – when it comes to matters of taste – you shouldn't rush to judgement.

Zizi Coin Coin is easy to drink – too easy you might say, and therein lies the problem. This refreshing little number slips down the throat effortlessly, carrying its charge of 10% alcohol by volume. A squeeze of fresh lemon, a few cubes of ice, and in the blink of an eye the bottle is empty. It should be noted that the manufacturers have thought it useful to distribute a version at 12% ABV in France, but I don't think the Belgians should take this personally. Size is not everything.

La Jupiler

So, how did the advertising wizards at Jupiler manage to put their finger on the subtle link between, on the one hand, men gathered around TV screens in a smoke-stained bar to watch the football championship and, on the other, those superfit whitewater rafters and mountaineers who feature in their adverts in their pursuit of thirst-quenching tins of beer?

In my humble opinion, the whole testosterone-filled publicity concept for this beer is something that could not possibly have been created by women, even given its cutting humour that pokes fun at the follies of masculinity. But it works! You need to know that 'la Jup' is our little nation's top-selling beer, far outstripping Stella and Maes Pils.

Produced in Liège at Jupille-sur-Meuse – hence the name – by the Piedboeuf brewery, which is now owned by the AB InBev giant (makers of Stella), Jupiler is in fact the youngest pils in the Belgian brewing landscape. It first saw light of day in 1966, when it was called Jupiler 5.

Packing a punch at 5.2% ABV, it can be sampled in virtually any Belgian bar worthy of the name. Its red and black label shows a bull, one of the symbols of Liège, now planted on all four feet, but originally standing on its hind legs. Ideally served on tap from the keg, the beer was supposed to reach the testicles of the rampant bull shown on the glass, with the head of foam above it rising to the rim. As the publicity slogan puts it, men know why.

A final detail that also conforms to the image: Jupiler produces a 5-litre 'barbecue special' cask, just to prove that, when it comes to our version of *vin de table*, the Belgians are not wimps. The integrated pressure pump may not always quite be up to the job, but this being a manly beer, what would you expect?

© belgiumtheplaceto.be TM - J Jeanmart

La Cuvée Ruffus
(Le Domaine des Agaises)

There is such a thing as Belgian wine. Ah yes, we are not a one-trick pony (beer)! Because production is on a small scale, and more or less *artisanal*, prices are relatively high, but the quality is very good – and shaped by the peculiarities of climate, soil and lesser-known grape varieties (Johanniter, Bronner, Solaris, Dornfelder, Muscaris, Regent) to give the wine the distinctive characteristics of *terroir*. The primary growing region is the Haspengouw (Hesbaye in French) in southern Flanders. But Wallonia is coming up fast on the inside lane, with vineyards along the River Meuse and in the southwest. The province of Namur, in particular, now produces attractive white, red and rosé wines under names that are building a following of dedicated fans, such as the Domaine viticole du Chenoy, Château de Bioul and the Domaine du Ry d'Argent.

But here I want to talk to you about a vineyard in the neighbouring province of Hainaut, at Haulchin to the west of Charleroi: Le Domaine des Agaises – producer of Cuvée Ruffus. Only trouble is, it's almost impossible to get hold of. Argggh! is what I would say at this point if I were you. But I insist for two reasons. One: the Belgians' excessive love of bubbles. We are the world's fifth largest market for Champagne, for example, accounting for almost one bottle per head per year. And in good years and bad, we consume over a million bottles of Cava, that well-known Spanish sparkler. And then there's French *crémant* and wines made by the *méthode traditionnelle* (as used to make Champagne), Italian *prosecco* and *spumante*, German *sekt*… basically, any excuse, and the Belgians pop open the fizz. Two: our mad, unshakeable desire to grow vines at any price to make our own wine – and because we used to have vineyards here, beginning in the Middle Ages, notably along the valley of the Meuse. Of course, as in most things alcoholic, it was the monks that started it: they needed wine for Communion.

© Rufus - Domaine des Agaises

Virtually every town was making wine for a while, but mini ice-ages and better trade connections with France, Germany and Spain undermined production, and by the 19th century the vineyards had all-but vanished. Three – ah, you weren't expecting that, were you! but this piece is all about the unexpected! Three: because, since the climate doesn't ever get that warm, sparking wines are seen as the best way to get the most out the environment on offer. The Agaises team may not be alone, indeed far from it, in producing wine in Belgium, but they make probably – hey, I'm going to stick my neck out here – undoubtedly (as things stand) the best wine in Belgium. Yup, no question about it, and what's more, one of the rare wines that can confidently take its place on the world stage without looking out of place. The vineyard stands on chalk, an afterthought of the Paris Basin, which – as we know – lends a little something to the Chardonnay vines planted in it. Yes, nudge, nudge, wink, wink – we're talking Champagne here. In short, their multi-award-winning *méthode traditionnelle* Cuvée Seigneur Ruffus, named after a one-time lord of the manor of the Agaises, is what in elevated circles is called *un must*. But you may have to be in elevated circles to buy it: its production of 100,000 bottles a year sells out virtually even before it is made.

La Bush

© belgiumtheplaceto.be TM - Eric Boschman

Holy Maria-Theresa, Empress of Austria, Sovereign of our Netherlands, what a temperament! But thank you! No, it's true: without this somewhat irascible little old bird, none of this would have happened, that's the truth of the matter. If she hadn't decided to suppress, in one fell stroke of the pen, all the old seigneurial breweries that had been exempt from tax – and hence luxuriating in unfair competitive advantage – the brewer and ancestral founder of the company, Joseph Leroy, would never have been able to cross the road, literally, to brew on his own account.

That was 1769, in the village of Pipaix, southeast of Tournai, where Bush beer is still brewed to this day at the oldest brewery in Wallonia – and one of the relatively few Belgian breweries that you can visit without being in a group. It's an independent family firm, still run by the Dubuisson family. Dubuisson means 'of the bush' – hence the name, adopted in 1933.

Bush beer is a symbol of a certain art of living in our provinces. When I was still an infant dribbling onto my parent's shoulder, from time to time I was allowed to suck on a finger dipped into the dense, foamy head. What a pleasure it was to see all those rubicund, luminous faces, their bawling mouths setting aflame the dark evenings of winter. Bush claims to be 'The Strongest Belgian Beer'. It is not alone in the claim, but hey, at 12% or 13% ABV – respect! Drinking one of these in full summer, outside on the terrace, really demands robust good health. But in winter, my goodness, it slips down a treat!

Dubuisson now produces about ten beers, including the line called Cuvée des Trolls, all in the upper stratosphere of 7–13% ABV. To celebrate the arrival of our Saviour in a dignified manner, why not treat yourself to a Bush de Noël (Christmas Bush)? I can picture the face of my Aunt Agatha when I said that I would be taking care of the Bush de Noël that year, and when I arrived with an armful of this magnificent amber-red beer. The faces of the whole family, in fact. Celebration!

La Blanche de Namur

Blanche de Namur was a dream of a princess, the daughter of Count Jean I of Namur. In 1334, when still a teenager, she received the attentions of the hunkily-named Magnus Eriksson, King of Norway and Sweden, who whisked her away to become his queen. All very fairytale stuff, which we can keep in mind as we raise our glass of the beer named 'in memory of her beauty, softness and delicacy'. And if the beer is a bit cloudy, so too is the rest of her rather murky story: poisonings, infidelity, plague. Heigh ho! it was the Middle Ages after all!

It so happens too that this famous beer is a *bière blanche* – a 'white beer', otherwise known as a 'wheat beer', for that is what it is made of. In this case: unmalted wheat, plus malted barley, and subtly flavoured with hops, coriander and bitter orange peel. It is also 'conditioned in the bottle' meaning that it goes on fermenting after bottling, to give it fizz – and it's the yeast that makes it cloudy. Don't call over the waiter to complain: that is how it is meant to be! In fact, the recommended way to serve Blanche de Namur is to half-fill your tall, tapering tumbler (the prescribed shape), then swill the bottle round to sweep up all the sediment before pouring the rest. It should be served cold, 2°C to 4°C – perfect for a summer's evening! But note: although 'light' by Belgian standards, it still comes in at 4.5% ABV. It is also the kind of beer that is drunk with a meal: a recommended accompaniment for robust fare, such as red meats, game and strong cheese.

Blanche de Namur is made at the charming old Du Bocq brewery in Purnode, in the heart of a wonderfully bucolic rural region called the Condroz. It was founded in 1858, and is now run by the sixth generation of the same family. Blanche de Namur is just one of several beers produced here, which include Triple Moine, Saison

1858, Deugniet (naughty 'Little Rascal', baring his bottom), Waterloo, St Benoît *(blonde* and *brune),* and its oldest brand La Gauloise *(blonde, brune* and *ambrée).* Also note, this is one of the rare breweries in Belgium that you can visit as an individual (as opposed to a group). Check out the schedule: in July and August it's open daily – the perfect time to sample a Blanche de Namur, perfectly served.

La Rochefort

At Rochefort, in the Province of Namur, there is an abbey – the Abbaye de Notre-Dame de Saint-Remy. There are 20 monks living happily – I trust – in this abbey. There is cheese, bread, there are crops and harvests. There are prayers and periods of contemplation, but there also a brewery. These monks are not like other monks: they are Trappist fathers and it is they who brew and process the delicious brown beer which I want to tell you about – a hand-crafted Trappist beer, made since 1595 and with a deliberately limited production in order to preserve quality. That said, the monks produce 30,000 litres of it a week. It's a brown beer of high fermentation, made entirely from natural ingredients: spring water, malt, hops, sugar, and yeast to orchestrate the fermentation. Refermented in the bottle, Rochefort delivers its full flavour only when served in its proper challice-shaped glass. Forget any other glass: that would spoil the moment and spoiling this pleasure is a sin which the Trappists might find hard to forgive.

The temperature at which the beer is served is also important. It should really be drunk at between 12° and 14° (i.e. cellar cool). Rochefort comes in three forms, and three degrees of alcoholic strength, numbered 6 (7.5% ABV), 8 (9.2% ABV) and 10 (11.3% ABV).

Rochefort 6 is my favourite. Burgundy in colour, yet clear. The head is firm, and the bubbles as big as my desire to lift the glass to my lips without delay. After its scent of deep, aromatic yeast comes its full-bodied, spicy flavour, with a slight sharpness and well-balanced bitterness. Enough talk. Good health!

© belgiumtheplaceto.be TM - J Jeanmart

Le Tango

The tango is a sensual and complex Argentinian dance of rare beauty, if it is well executed. To the sound of a *bandoneón* (concertina), a man and a woman intertwine their legs, their arms, their fingers, their eyes, and celebrate life, death and love. Modern tango is even more sensual that the old. Quicker, expressing all at once the pride of the hildalgo sad to be separated from his roots and the man born in this corner of the Americas, far from the Europe of his fantasies. The tango is also a way of chasing out the grey of daily life, and the country's recent years of darkness. Tango is the art of living, a way of life, a way – quite simply – of being. A tango dancer, in his daily existence, can be old, grey-haired, ugly and stooped. When the music begins, he becomes once more that person that he dreamt of being one day, standing upright and, with his dark and pin-sharp eyes, gazing with disdain upon a mundane world. Tango is all of that. It can also be a telephone company in Luxembourg. But, anyway, tell me this: who can explain why the subtle mix of pils with grenadine at the bottom that fuels student nights – and all those other raucous student drinking-and-singing events which the Belgians call *guindailles* (especially in Le Carré in Liège) – might carry this name? Does it refer to that familiar gaze of drinkers after 12 such tangos? That gaze which peers uncomprehendingly at a mundane world before quietly throwing up in the gutter?

Or is it because of the delicate movements of the fingers running along the fluting at the bottom of the pils glass? Or because of the filaments of carmine-red syrup which dance in the depths of the glass and the different strata throughout the full height of the beer? Or was it simply on account of the raffish nature of the mixture, a bold and carefree gesture which flies in the face of conformity?

© belgiumtheplaceto.be TM - J Jeanmart

Le Cercueil
(or Mazout)

This is the dark counterpart of the Tango (see previous page), and if you haven't read that page already, I suggest you do so now. There, so you're back again! Tango is sort-of red, because it's pils with a shot of grenadine. *Le cercueil* is sort-of black, as its name suggests (it means 'coffin'), because it is made of beer mixed with cola, to no particular formula. It is sometimes also known as *mazout* (the kind of fuel oil you put in stoves). It's a name particularly associated with the town of Mouscron, in the province of Hainaut, where the drink may also be called *maz,* or *taz,* or *tazmataz.* But given the horrible price of petrocarbons these days, I think I'll stick with the coffin.

Our French friends are not above this kind of thing, but instead of beer they mix wine or pastis with various sweet things. Their famous *blanc limé* (white wine with lemonade) or *perroquet* (pastis with *sirop de menthe* (mint syrup)) have very few adversaries in the world of good taste, so I'm told. With us, it's the blondes that we like to dye, and *blonde* beers at that. Come to think of it, maybe this desire to tinker with the natural is some kind of extension of a fascination for hair dye – which happens also to fixate many among *le cercueil's* target age group: adolescents.

Both *le cercueil* and tango serve a similar social function: a rite of passage. After the age of about 14, however, it gets a bit difficult to order a *cercueil* without seeming a bit of a plonker. But these low(ish)-alcohol mixed drinks do at least give young people a way to become familiar with beer. After the first bout of binge-drinking comes the first hangover, and the first efforts to master the effects of consumption. All part of the learning process, which must surely be a good thing. And with a name like *le cercueil,* no one can say they haven't been warned!

© belgiumtheplaceto.be TM - J Jeanmart

The non-alcoholic ones:

Spa mineral water

Spa, a town of myth and legend, which has given its name – known throughout the world – to bubbling baths and health resorts. That's a bit strange, isn't it? For those to whom this comes as some surprise, it has to be said that, Spa, a good century ago, was rather more than the Sleeping Beauty that it is today. The Tsar of Russia came to take the waters in this town in eastern Belgium, arriving in his private train. Numerous crowned heads of state sojourned here. The great King Léopold II of the Belgians would spend months in Spa. Ah, yes, those were the days Belgium counted for more in the world than it does today, you would have to say.

At Spa the water is just not like it is anywhere else. Today people still come here to take the waters, and above all to take a spa. You come to Spa to do yourself good: a bit of hydrotherapy, a bit of massage, a bit of fresh air among the forest, but above all, sinking into copper baths surrounded by millions of bubbles. After that, drinking cup in hand, you head for the numerous *pouhons* located around the town. *Pouhons*? What's that? 'Springs' to the rest of us, but it's much more fun to say *pouhons*, and besides that's 100% local. So, you head for one of the town's *pouhons* and you quaff the water. Water which has such a distinctive taste, so low in minerals that it has a texture that can sometimes be quite startling.

Spa mineral water has been bottled and sold since the 16th century.

Today the brand is owned by the Spadel Group. I don't know the historic reasons for the colour coding used for their labels, but it has successfully infiltrated into public consciousness, to the extant that when many people want sparkling mineral water they simply ask for 'Spa rouge'.

Le Cécémel

I have just noticed that most products that we Belgians are fond of as children are either yellow or red. Most, if perhaps not all. There's the cow of the Milka brand, but we'll pretend not to notice her: she's mauve. That's a bit weird, isn't it? We can make the Belgian flag (black, yellow, red) if we use the black liquorice bears and mice (which we always eat last, and which thus always remain longest in the packet). For the red we have Mignonettes (see page 89), the packaging of LU *spéculoos,* strawberries, grenadine, and Materne strawberry jam (see page 94).

For the yellow, I suggest: Kwatta chocolate spread and sprinkles, *bonbons* Napoléon (see page 29), the illustrated and comic book characters Maya the bee and Marsupilami, and of course Cécémel. Make no bones about it, Cécémel is *'le seul vrai'* (the only authentic one); it's written on the bottle. The glass bottle predates its Tetra Pak packaging by a long chalk, and can still be found – it's much more fun to shake than those opaque cartons where you can't see the chocolate mixing with the milk.

What has always fascinated me is the *sucre de raisin* (literally, 'grape sugar') listed among the ingredients. It's something that makes me think it is good for one's health, like the grape juice that you can buy at pharmacies for people who are ill. Now I know it's just another word for dextrose, but heigh-ho!

You can get 'Cécémel light' now, and I find that really disappointing. For me, Cécémel was always a drink for the sporty types; cartons labelled 'Energy' feature mountainbikers and skateboarders in full cry. So Cécémel *light* – how's that going to give you the energy boost you expect? Only as far as the bus stop. If that!

© belgiumtheplaceto.be TM - J Jeanmart

La grenadine

© belgiumtheplaceto.be TM - J Jeanmart

I have got to tell you about drinking bottles (*gourdes* in French), faithful friend of all young adventurers in their shorts. In the heads of these proud kids, its only rival in the life-and-death struggle for survival is the multi-bladed penknife. However, as you know, a boy will be thirsty at every moment of his life, and only has a true sense of reassurance if, at the start of an expedition, he feels the means of his salvation dangling heavily from his belt. If I have to take a little time (and God knows I have plenty of other things I should be doing!) to paint the picture of this concept for you, it's to help you appreciate the ideal content of such a drinking bottle, and the place this holds in the life of a man: grenadine. For it never enters the head of any parents worthy of the name to fill the *gourdes* of their offspring with a half-litre of coffee (in which case, we'd be talking about a thermos), or buttermilk, or pure malt whisky, or even plain water. It's grenadine (diluted to taste) or nothing – adding a bit of flavour to this journey through the woods, as well as a dose of calories. Allow me to digress a moment. Grenadine *light* is an abomination, and if the general drift of what I have to say touches you in any way, I beg you never to buy it. Thank you.

So what is grenadine? Originally it was a syrup made from pomegranates (*grenades* in French), a fruit originally cultivated in Persia and India, and later throughout the Mediterranean region. True pomegranate syrup has a slightly softer and less tangy taste than modern grenadines, which are made from a mixture of red fruits such as blackcurrants, redcurrants, elderberries and raspberries, depending on the brand. But the flavours of pomegranate syrup and that of red fruits are similar enough, and the latter can even be as 'natural' as true pomegranate syrup, contrary to the fanatical claims of the organics brigade who sometimes fall a bit short of reason. It can happen to anyone. Even to me, I assure you, albeit that I am a model of open-mindedness. . Listen, I have been drinking grenadine all my life and have come to no harm. Scouts' honour! And although I now no longer walk through the woods with my gang so often, it still somehow reminds me of that glorious boyhood spirit of adventure.

Le Liégeois

The story I'm going to tell you is now known only to rare individuals whose number barely exceeds that of the last surviving *'poilus'* – the rank-and-file soldiers of the First World War. It was people with old-fashioned names like Hildegarde, Aloïs, Romain and Marie-Paule who maintained the legend, and now it's just you and me. You'll have to listen carefully: I'm inclined to mumble. At that time, making war was a habit. People went to war like now they go to a football match. At the drop of a hat they took their red sashes out of their wardrobes and began chanting their victory songs the moment their troop started marching down the road. Alas, victory was not always the outcome, and while they forced themselves to forget as quickly as possible the thrashings of the past, these continued to haunt the depths of the hearts of the brave – even those of the famously valiant Liégeois. These ardent men of La Ville Ardente (as Liège is known) struggled ceaselessly to prove their valour. Until the day when fortune smiled upon them at last.

Their lucky star came in the form of a grumpy curate. This was at the end of the 18th century, on the eve of the Liège Révolution (1789–95), which unseated the Prince-Bishops after eight centuries of autocratic rule. While the fire of their zeal smouldered, the morale of the combatants peaked and troughed like a sawblade, sometimes strong enough to move mountains, sometimes barely strong enough to raise a glass of *pékèt* to their lips. 'Enough!' bellowed our man of the cloth. 'What are you? Wimps or *valeureux Liégeois?'* And soon, seized by a divine anger and threatening them with the fires of hell, he smashed all their bottles of *pékèt* and replaced them with a potion of his own devising. The effect was immediate. Our soldiers straightened up, jumped to their feet, chests bulging with a new energy, ready to grapple with the worst of enemies.

The legend of les *valeureux Liégeois* was born. What was in that magic potion? After the death of the priest, the miraculous recipe was found between two pages of the Holy Bible. Homemade orangeade into which is added a smidgen of explosive from the artillery grenades hidden in a false seat in the confessional. All that remained was to go into commercial production. The priest's powder did not last long, and besides, times had changed: it seemed just as good to add grenadine to the orangeade, so a convenient bit of wordplay came to the rescue. *Grenade* is also the French word for pomegranate – indeed the first was inspired by the second. So instead of extract of grenade, extract of pomegranate – otherwise known as grenadine – was used, creating the drink we now know as *liégeois*.

Well, it's true if you believe it. I believe it because *liégeois* should be drunk with the eyes of a child, marvelling at the colour, then closing them as you let the scented bubbles fizz on your tongue.

13. A food fight!

Les Boulettes sauce tomate vs les boulets sauce lapin

Boulettes sauce tomate: meatballs in tomato sauce. Well made, this is delicious, flavoursome comfort food at its best. The balls are made of the ground meat as used in *pain de viande* (see page 122), rolled to whatever size takes your fancy, coated in breadcrumbs, fried, then immersed in a homemade tomato sauce and served on a heap of buttery mashed potato. It's a classic dish, a regular feature of children's menus up and down the country – guaranteeing loyalty for life.

Boulets sauce lapin: meatballs in rabbit sauce. It's a bit like *entrecôte sauce crevettes* – steak with shrimp sauce. Shock! Horror! No, let me explain. The best thing that goes with shrimps is a good shrimp sauce, i.e. mayonnaise. But the good people of Liège, who do everything differently (like their spelling of *boulettes*) have decided that the same sauce goes well with entrecôte steak, hence entrecôte sauce crevettes, but without a shrimp in sight. The same goes for *Boulets sauce lapin:* it uses a classic sauce for rabbit, but rest assured, no bunnies were harmed for your meatballs. Herewith the proof of it:

© OPT - Emmanuel Mathez

- In a pan, fry the meatballs so they take colour on all the surfaces; remove. Deglaze the pan with vinegar and sugar; reduce by half, then add onions, thyme, bayleaves and marjoram.
- Put the meatballs back on this bed of onions and add water to half-cover.
- Cook for 20 minutes.
- Remove the meatballs, mix the sauce, pick up your pot of Sirop de Liège (see page 131) and add two teaspoons of this nectar, plus 40 raisins, and not a single raisin more.
- Serve with chips (frites). And don't forget to wipe your lips before you drink: this sauce makes more of a mess on the rim of a glass than fuchsia-coloured lipstick.

Les chicons braisés vs les chicons au gratin

I've got to admit it straight out: I have a weakness for *chicons*. That's those linguistically elusive, little white and pale green torpedo-shaped salady things variously known as chicory or Belgian endives in English, and *witloof* in Dutch. I would happily eat them every day, given half the chance.

Chicons are strange and delicate things. They are spouts from the roots of *chicorée* lettuce, an invented vegetable first discovered by accident by a botanist working in Schaerbeek, Brussels, in around 1840. Buried in soil in open ground, they grow in the dark, hence their colour. Be wary of foreign endives that are produced on an industrial scale in hot, dark sheds and fed hydroponically.

In my opinion, *chicons braisés* (braised chicons) is the finest vegetable dish ever. Well, tell me if you know of any other that has such a soft and juicy flavour offset by that piquant, moreish bitterness.

To make perfect *chicons braisés,* you don't need much, but a few things are indispensable. Good salted butter, fresh and perky *chicons*. My father grew *chicons* in the cellar, in the dark, in a huge basin filled with earth. In my childhood this impressed me, and I avoided going there because this mysterious thing frightened me in some vague way. Then children and *chicons* – that's something that does not always go together. Before braising, the *chicons* have to be cooked slowly in a little melted butter under a sheet of greaseproof paper. Patience is essential. If you have only 15 minutes to spare, forget it: you'll end up with carbonised shells surrounding a soggy interior. It is only when the *chicons* are cooked through, and not before, that you start the braising proper, in a covered pan over a high flame. Just add salt and pepper, nothing else. Hmm… just thinking about it…

© belgiumtheplaceto.be TM - J Jeanmart

Chicons au gratin: it's a like a marriage – for better or for worse. The best *Chicons au gratin* are made by your grandmother, or aunt, or mother. *Chicons au gratin* made for schools, university dining halls and army canteens are often the worst.

- First braise your *chicons* (see above); drain and set aside, preserving the cooking liquid.
- Roll each in a thin slice of lean ham
- Place in a baking dish and cover with béchamel sauce made with 75gm of roux (flour and butter) for every litre of cooking liquid from the *chicons*.
- Place in the oven for a few minutes until the top turns golden. Call everyone to the table, bibs on, and serve while piping hot. How good is that!

La couque vs le baulus

'Bonjour. I would like three butter *couques* – yes, not too well-done – two with chocolate and two with raisins.'

'But what are these *couques* that you are talking about?' asks a foreign friend who has accompanied me to the baker.

It is true that the word *'couque'* in Belgium can mean a lot of very different things, depending on the region. The *couques de Dinant* (see page 48), for instance, are rock-hard biscuits. But my sort of *couques* are soft and flaky; the chocolate one is called a *'pain au chocolat'* across the border in France, and the raisin one a *'pain aux raisins.'* The plain one resembles a croissant, but is sweeter and firmer. It has an inimitable flavour, to the extent that I have heard Belgians abroad complain that they can't get hold of anything like them. Generally they are eaten plain, but there's nothing to stop you adding a layer of butter and a spoonful of jam. Strong coffee is the classic accompaniment. The *couque aux raisins* is more or less the same, but for its generous sprinkling of currants, and the *couque au chocolat* is peppered with little balls of chocolate.

A *baulus* is something else again. I have always had a fatal weakness for them, and unfortunately they had a fatal attraction to my hips and the spare tyres that garlanded my thickening frame from an early age. Only by stringent remedial action was I able to regain my shape and finally returned to eating *baulus* without self-recrimination. A *baulus* is nothing like a *couque aux raisins,* which it resembles on paper only. The pastry is a sublime confection of flour, butter with a little lard, eggs, yeast, sugar, milk and salt, topped by *crème pâtissière,* raisins or other dried fruit and a sprinkling of brown sugar. Every mouthful has a meltingly soft centre. My father would buy a huge one, the size of a tart, every Friday to share among the family. Alas they are hard to come by these days: if you ever see one in a baker's window, do not hesitate.

© belgiumtheplaceto.be TM - J Jeanmart

Les boudins de Liège – all of them!

Let's be straight here. We're not talking about *boudin* in the sense that is sometimes used disparagingly – and, oh, so unfairly – to refer to certain over-generous feminine body shapes that are, shall we say, somewhat unappealingly under-generously dressed. That would in any case be hypothetical in the context of Liège, which is known for the lithe beauty and *'sexyness'* (as they say in French) of its women. No, here we are talking about charcuterie, in the strict sense of the term.

Boudin blanc (white sausage) is made in various ways in different parts of Europe. Without being exhaustive, we could cite: the Belgian Ardennes and the French Ardennes (especially at Rethel); in France, Normandy (Avranches, Le Havre), Nièvre; Catalonia and Bavaria. It's essentially a preparation made with white minced meat (pork, poultry, veal), onions, eggs, fresh breadcrumbs, milk and a mixture of herbs and spices.

But *boudin blanc* is also – and most particularly – a speciality of Liège. Its historical roots go back to the days of the Prince-Bishopric of Liège in the Middle Ages. At that time it was a kind of gruel made of milk, bread, animal fat and bits of chicken and ham. It was a comforting, family dish, eaten at Christmas on return from Midnight Mass. Subsequently this gruel was improved and refined so it could be stuffed into pig's intestines to give it the oblong shape of a sausage.

Today *boudin blanc de Liège* is made with a carefully judged blend of lean pork and fatty pork (2/3 to 1/3 respectively), onions, eggs, fresh breadcrumbs, milk, salt, pepper, nutmeg, thyme, parsley and, above all, marjoram. It is the marjoram that distinguishes *boudin blanc de Liège* from all others.

© belgiumtheplaceto.be TM - J Jeanmart

It's eaten cold, with bread, or alternatively cut into slices and quickly pan-fried. It can also be added as an ingredient to soups, terrines, sandwiches, savoury tarts, quiches, or served as an apéritif snack with a little Belgian piccalilli, or mustard, or horseradish sauce on the side, to dip it into. Or why not go totally *liégeois* and serve it with some Sirop de Liège – quick, simple and wondrously good!

The people of Liège – gloriously extrovert, generous and creative – have been busy developing the art of serving their *boudin blanc* since the origin of the recipe in medieval times. During the New Year festivities, classic *boudin blanc* will be presented at Liégeois tables alongside its cousins: *boudin vert* (green, made with cabbage), and others made with raisins, or nuts, or hazelnuts, or – sweeter – crushed *spéculoos* biscuits. There's no limit to the imaginative invention applied, with unexpected gastronomic results. Keep your eyes peeled when you visit the Christmas markets of Brussels or Wallonia: it's not unusual to find specialist stalls devoted entirely to these *boudins liégeois de Noël*.

Index

© La Quincaillerie

Tourist destination introduction: Françoise Scheepers

Photographs: Joseph Jeanmart, Jean-Luc Flémal, Emmanuel Mathez, Philippe Lermussiaux, Jon Martin, Willy Coppens, La pâtisserie Eggenols - Liège, Ruffus - Domaine des Agaises, Oliver Knight, Lionel Lo[illegible]ckx - Viva Mboma - Brussels, Couques Collard - Dinant, Nick Haslam, John Brunton, Boulangerie Vienne - Tournai, OPT Avantage, Jean-Paul Remy, Laurent Gerbaud, La Quincaillerie - Brussels, Cedric Sophie and Eric Boschmann

Front Cover artwork: Martine Scheffen · Cartoon illustrations: Kevin White
Design and Artwork: GreenApple Graphics

Published by Racine in cooperation with the
Belgian Tourist Office Brussels & Wallonia

EAN: 9782873868277 · Copyright Registration: D.2013.6852.1
Legal Deposit: November 2013 · Printed in Spain

Belgian Tourist Office
Brussels • Wallonia

Racine